The Savior's Perfect Yoke

POWER HOUSE

The Savior's Perfect Yoke

Approaching the Work from a Posture of Rest

How to find relief, refreshment, and recreation for your soul while serving your Kingdom purpose.

Stephen Everett

Published by: **Power House**

An imprint of Power House Studios LLC.

 thepowerhousestudio.com

PO Box 101678

Cape Coral FL 33910

Home of *The Power House Blueprint*™ Concierge Publishing System

Preface

With this first book in a series of leadership development tools, we invite you to embark on a journey of discovery and dominion in the Kingdom of God. This series of books was birthed from teaching sessions during our God's Kingdom Leaders' Summits ™. It seems good to preface the release (here in the first book of many) answering the obvious question, "Why would leaders need to spend time to study foundational truths?" Some may wonder, "Isn't this an evangelistic message to the lost, to those who do not know Christ?" Or, perhaps, "Shouldn't leaders already be well-versed in these doctrines?" Let's answer those questions here in the Preface.

In the most significant global shift in the past 500 years, beginning in 2020, God orchestrated a divine halt that will affect all the times to come. He caused a recalibration in the worldwide scope of every area of influence. Amid worldly chaos, He worked all things together for our good. At the direction of His Voice, we've had a reset, had to reload, and are in preparation for a relaunch. So, this is like a global "re-" season. The Father intended to ease our church-made religious burdens by reinstalling His intent.

Consequently, Michelle and I are impressed in our spirits that we need to revisit the foundational doctrines of the Kingdom of God in an extended teaching series. Did you know that in Deuteronomy 31:10–13, God commanded the priests and people to rehearse (rehear or revisit) the foundations of the law every seven years? Many different vocations require their labor force to do this in the modern workforce. It is one of the better ways to keep workers up to date and maintain the best skill level. It is called ***continuing education*** and is required in many fields to maintain licensing to practice that vocation. *How much more should we pursue continuing education in the doctrines of the Kingdom of God?*

It is in that spirit (and in agreement with the Scripture in Matthew 6:33) that we are led to begin releasing this series of books for the continuing education of ministry leaders, marketplace leaders, teams and staff, and lay people who desire to further their development in The Word.

You may find that the dialogue is different from our previous books. The text contained in this series is taken directly from live leaders' intensives, so it will often present as very conversational, filled with practical application and plain language.

For example, you may frequently encounter direct questions to the reader in the text or see the instruction to *Selah.* "Selah" means to pause and ponder. You are encouraged to do so. Take a break—as much time as needed—to meditate on the thoughts, beliefs, or patterns presented that may have been new or even old ones that are being renewed or challenged by clear examination of scripture. Each chapter was taken from one session in our apostolic schools of ministry. You may benefit by taking a break between chapters to really study out the material and to hear what Holy Spirit would provide light on.

Michelle and I pray you are blessed on your journey of discovery and dominion. We invite you to join us in person for future God's Kingdom Leaders' Summits.

Contents

CHAPTER ONE

COME UNTO ME

Come unto me, all ye that labour and are heavy
laden, and I will give you rest. Take my yoke upon
you, and learn of me; for I am meek and lowly
in heart: and ye shall find rest unto your souls.
For my yoke is easy, and my burden is light.
Matthew 11:28–30

An opportunity of a lifetime has just been announced. No other person on earth could make such an offer. What will we do with it? Jesus offered a change to humanity that required a response from each person. In these passages in Matthew, He said, "Come unto me." This was an invitation to place the hearer into a better position in life—a position producing powerful transformation.

Rather than considering these verses alone, it is important to view the earlier events of Matthew 11. A fuller view of the text is necessary before drawing our conclusions. Let's go back to the beginning of the chapter. (We note that the scripture did not originally happen in chapters, but that is where we will begin for now.) It was mainly activities, conversations, teachings, preaching, and visiting different cities.

It begins with a couple of John's disciples approaching Jesus. We see in Matthew 11:3 they said to him, "Are You the Coming One, or do we look for another?" (NKJV) This question is profound. It is even more so because it is still being asked by many today, albeit with slightly different wording. Here is an example: Is this really what God is doing on the earth? Or are we to look for something else? That's the way it unfolds in a modern mindset. In the first century, Jesus was the manifestation of what God was doing on earth. But in the Greek language, this verse says more to us. From the Greek, the whole idea of "the coming one" is "Are you the Ever-coming One?" Selah. The answer was and still is, "Yes!"

This is an important detail. Get this. We see this name of the Lord in The Revelation when He introduced Himself. He said, "I'm the one that is, and was, and is to come" (Revelation 1:4, 8). In the Old Testament, this was the name we now pronounce, "Yahweh." That rendering meant, "I'm always the coming one, but you have to discern how I'm coming."

And that's the key, a very vital key, to discern how He's coming. So, throughout the Word, Jesus is identified as The One, the Always Coming One. We must adjust our view of

Him coming to align with this truth. We must realize He comes in various ways and will come multiple times as The One, the Always Coming One. And the ever-coming One invites us to come to Him as ever-coming ones.

In this invitation, Jesus brings up the matter of rest. There are certainly many who are asking the Lord for some semblance of rest right now. That's always been something that humanity should have searched out because the rest, the seventh day, was the initial full day of humankind on the earth. It was hard-wired, so to speak, into our design. Father God always intended for humans to live life *from* the posture of rest. It was never to be go, go, go, and work, work, work until nothing was left in our vast arsenal. And by the time you get to Jesus, conservatively 4000 years later, He acknowledges that creation needs rest.

Jesus is not speaking of laziness and slothfulness but rest. It's a rest that springs from humanity's interior to the exterior. Then in Matthew 11:29, he said, "Take my yoke upon you and learn of me," or learn from me. He is opening the truth to them (and us) about what will happen as we fulfill the dominion mandate out of our posture of rest.

Here is the follow-up thought in that lesson: if you try to satisfy the dominion mandate any other way, it will wear you out. Life will become heavy, burdensome, and mainly filled with labor and sorrow. In John 6:65, he said, "Therefore said I unto you, that no man can come unto Me, except it were given unto him of My Father."

Back to Matthew 11, as they (we) are drawing near, He said, "For I am meek." Now he begins to describe himself. He begins to describe the posture in which it is best to learn. He said, "For I am meek and lowly in heart" (v. 29). Please understand that meekness is not weakness, but is actually a strength. It means that one is balanced and not governed by emotional highs and lows. You could underscore meekness and humility as the best postures in which to learn. And then he said, "And [in that posture of humility and learning] you shall find rest." And finally, he said in your taking his yoke," you will find "my yoke is easy, and my burden is light" (v.30).

That's what I will focus on in these next several chapters. How do you take the yoke? What is the yoke all about? But before that, we must ask, "Why would we need to revisit this in a leaders' series? Isn't this an evangelistic message to the lost, to those who do not know Christ?" Let's answer that!

In the most significant global shift in the past 500 years, beginning in 2020, God orchestrated a divine halt that will affect all the times to come. He caused a recalibration in the worldwide scope of every area of influence. Amid worldly chaos, He worked all things together for our good. At the direction of His Voice, we've had a reset, had to reload, and are in preparation for a relaunch. So, this is like a global "re-" season. The Father intended to ease our church-made religious burdens by reinstalling His intent.

So, yes, generally, you will often hear this passage when inviting people to come to the Lord for the first time. But there's more to this than our evangelistic experience. The invitation to come into an initial relationship with Jesus is of foremost importance, but there is more to experience beyond that. He is the Ever-coming One, remember? And as He is, so are we in this world. (That's found in 1 John 4:17.) We are ever-coming and developing an ever-growing and greater understanding and application of the scriptures.

And so, in our text in Matthew 11, Jesus is saying that there's a yoke involved, and only through taking his yoke will you find rest. It is not an option. We're discovering many things that are not an option if one desires to fulfill our Kingdom mandate or assignments. Our assignment can be fulfilled if we answer two questions: **Who are we? And, why are we here?**

The last thing we should want is to leave the earth without discovering what we were here for and what God's Kingdom is all about. Your Kingdom mandate (the whole of your assignments) is the reality God purposed you to fulfill.

And then second to that would be to discover your purpose and not pursue it. And so, this discovery involves taking the yoke and finding rest for your soul. So clearly, this first phase of His rest will calm your spirit. And then, as you engage, your soul is further developed. When we develop and mature, as we free the soul from stress and a lack of rest, we move rapidly toward vast new discoveries in God.

Jesus said, "you will find rest for your souls. For my yoke is easy, and my burden is light" (vv. 29 – 30). Now bear that in mind. As you're reading and discovering details, he didn't say there won't be a burden. That's not what he said.

Although this may be a familiar passage to many of you, I hadn't done much preaching or teaching on this passage in more than forty years. You can see why it was necessary to revisit this, or at least it was for me. The Lord drew me to deeply ponder this passage over many months. I have discovered much as I took a fresh look at it.

There's always something fresh because it's the word coming out of The Word's mouth. It's what I call the *universality* aspect and its *particularity*. That means that it covers each age, but it's also unique for the moment. Thus, you have the eternal aspect.

If you think you have discovered everything that could be said or shared about a passage, you've just deceived yourself. Paul said in 1 Corinthians 8:2, "And if any man think that he knoweth any thing, he knoweth nothing yet as he ought to know." So we must train ourselves to hear and receive the Word of God as fresh bread every time.

Let's continue as we define some of these words. I love what Lamentations 3:27 says: "It is good for a man that he bear the yoke in his youth." This word for youth is your state of juvenility; as a juvenile, it is good to bear a *yoke.* Another version says, "It is good for a man to bear the yoke from his youth" (CJB). That means you should never *stop* bearing the yoke. In remaining yoked, there is no opportunity to run wild and fulfill one's own agenda. Jesus gives this invitation for our benefit—I especially love this because most of what you experience in God is generally by invitation.

In The Revelation, do you know or do you remember what The Lord said to John? "Come up hither" (Rev. 4:1, 11:12). That's the invitation. You don't just barge into eternal and heavenly things; mysteries require an invitation. The throne-rooms of even natural kings and queens follow this pattern of honor—one enters by invitation only. (And, not without a gift.)

Later, He said, not only, "Come up hither," but He then said, "Come hither [come closer]" (Rev. 21:9). He wants to show you specific things, like the mystery of iniquity (2 Thessalonians 2:7) and the mystery of the Lamb's wife (Rev. 21:9). These revelations require coming close to Him. His invitation was, "Come to me, come up close."

Do you hear Him right now? Can you hear Him saying this to us (the body of Christ) right now? Yes, it is true. If you want your life to rise out of the muck and mire—what we might call (in modern terminology) the swamp of everyday trials, tests, and tragedies—and into clouds of glorious victory in life, then you've got to come up! You must come up!

To truly thrive, not merely survive, we must answer the invitation and show up with our gift, our yielded lives!

Now, back to our original text in Matthew 11: "Come to Me, all you who labor and are heavy laden, and I will give you rest" (v. 28). Let's look at the word *labor*. In this passage, labor means feeling fatigued, working hard, and toiling. I want to establish that it was always the mind of God that man in this earthly environment would work and have dominion. Genesis 2:15 says, "And the Lord God took the man, and put him into the garden of Eden to dress it and to keep it." So we see that work wasn't something that he engaged in just because he disobeyed God. No. The added aspect in work once man disobeyed was *toil.*

7

And unto Adam he said, Because thou hast hearkened unto the voice of thy wife, and hast eaten of the tree, of which I commanded thee, saying, Thou shalt not eat of it: cursed is the ground for thy sake; in sorrow shalt thou eat of it all the days of thy life;

Thorns also and thistles shall it bring forth to thee; and thou shalt eat the herb of the field;

In the sweat of thy face shalt thou eat bread, till thou return unto the ground; for out of it wast thou taken: for dust thou art, and unto dust shalt thou return. (Genesis 3:17–19)

But *before* the introduction to struggle, man's work was the work of discovery and dominion!

God placed everything in the environment strategically to teach man something about himself. The moment man disconnected from God because of disobedience, he placed himself into a new position. As Ecclesiastes describes it, his work would now be labor and sorrow rather than labor and joy. Jesus acknowledged that humanity had experienced tremendous labor and toil, producing weariness. He showed them the only way out of it. Jesus employed the original intent: discovery! It was about discovering their solution because they searched for ways out of life's hard, heavy labor (like so many are still today). He said, "The only way out of it is to come to me."

And then, from our primary text in Matthew 11, we have "heavily laden" (v. 28). In all that God has placed around us, there is a picture of instruction as to who He is. Every detail tells us how the Kingdom of God works. We can understand that both the Greek and the Hebrew languages are picturesque, which often means a word, or an alphabet character, will communicate a picture.

For example, recently, in the God's Kingdom Leadership Summit and on the television broadcasts, we taught about the insight (the revelation) within the descriptive letters and words that form the number of each year. We investigated the Hebrew Aleph-Bet (the Hebraic alphabet). The picture for the decade, particularly the opening of the decade beginning in 2020, was the mouth. And then the previous year, for example, the letter was the sixteenth in the aleph-bet, and the picture was the eye. So, a single word or letter gives you a picture to store in your image-nation.

Where am I going with this? In our passage in Matthew, we have this type of visual. And here in this picture, he's saying, like loaded pack animals or vessels, we are loaded beyond what we can carry. Jesus is sharing this to give a spiritual picture of being *heavy-laden*. It is to be overburdened with spiritual anxiety. Forward movement will be stunted if you remain overloaded and overburdened with anxiety. Jesus said, "In rest, I will refresh you." So releasing His Word and refreshing is essential to what we want to accomplish in this series.

Continuing with the phrase, "Take my yoke" (v. 29), the word *yoke* is engaging because it is the Greek word *zygos*[1] (pronounced "zugos"). And the idea that it conveys is *to be joined.* Keep that in mind, *joined.* Our first joining is to The Lord. "He who is joined to the Lord is one spirit" (1 Corinthians 6:17). The scripture doesn't say one flesh, but we are one spirit because God is spirit (John 4:24).

To be clear, let us establish that God designed the fleshly bodies for our sojourn here. Our physical body gives us a house to function on this earth. But our original joining was to the Lord who gave us life. When sin entered in through humans' disobedience, sin prevented us from joining God. We are redeemed when we come again to Him, born-again, reconciled to the Lord, receiving His salvation! We are redeemed—rejoined to God's original life-giving, burden-removing, (heavy) yoke-destroying power! We are joined to the Savior's perfect yoke!

Here's another fact about a yoke. A yoke is equally a coupling. In the Strong's Concordance, it is G2218: *zygós*, which is "a yoke; a wooden bar placed over the neck of a pair of animals so they can pull together; (figuratively) what unites (joins) two people to move (work) together as one.²"

We call husband and wife a couple. Or, if someone is courting and intend to become man and wife, one might say, "Look at that couple!" In a covenant marriage, they become yoked together as one. In Spirit, you are joined, intimately coupled with God, Elohim, your creator. When you are born again, accepting Christ as Lord and Savior, you are reconciled, yoked, joined, coupled with Him. When the Holy Spirit inhabits us, we are joined to Him. Thus, we are joined to the Trinity. (See this clearly in 1 Corinthians 6:17.) It is equally important to grasp that in that reconciliation, that joining in Christ, you are dis-joined and unyoked from the body of burdens, heavy toil, and death!

So, we see that it is powerful to be coupled. It matters to whom and what we couple ourselves. It must be more than, "Oh, doesn't that couple look good together?" It's much deeper than that. So, as I get into it, the yoke has one more definition: a pair of balances. *Zygós* unites two elements to work as one unit. For example, when two pans (weights) operate together on a balance scale, that's called a yoke. A pair of oxen pulling a single plow is a yoke as well.

In every sense, Jesus was saying when you take his yoke, that's what you get. You get the opportunity to be joined, to move in couples; you become anointed pairs of balancing elements. Isn't it interesting how he released the early apostles in pairs? They went out by twos. This can be seen with Peter and John and Barnabas and Saul. Then later, when Saul became Paul, the joining became apostles and prophets. Paul, an apostle, and Silas, a prophet, labored together. The scripture said that specifically.

So, as a balancing pair, you have the apostle and the prophet working together. I've heard people say, and I've also said, that two apostles rarely work together because you have two authorities. Unfortunately, they try to "one-up" or "out authority" each other. But seriously, all it requires is humbling, disciplining, and training yourself to realize when the operation of grace is on the other! Then, you could continue to work

11

together. Come on. Our oneness is to be in His Image, and the model of being "joined in Christ," as Christ in the earth. As He is, so am I, so are we, in this earth.

We find Jesus, in Matthew 23, having that conversation. To paraphrase portions of the chapter, the disciples were vying for position. They were trying to figure out, "All right, who will be in charge once he leaves?" The heart of Jesus' reply was, "The first thing I want you to remember is that you're all brothers." That's first. "Although you are all in the developmental phase of the apostolic gifting and grace, some will teach, some will shepherd (pastor), some may serve in other ways, but don't forget that the equipping is all God, and you are brothers serving others." Apostles can only work together successfully when they think this way. It can be done. But again, humbling ourselves is the key, along with being willing to be the portion we're ordained to be and not trying to be every portion. One will be relieved of huge burdens and much anxiety when that action step of faith (believing and acting on it) is practiced!

As Jesus said, "You will find rest when you learn of me," we see an intermission from labor that is given. In sports like basketball, you play two halves, with an intermission in between. American football is the same way; you have two different halves. What's the purpose of intermission? You're going to rest! Secondly, you reflect on what you've done during the first half. If it's not working, you need to develop a different strategy.

I watch our eldest grandsons playing high school football every Friday night when I get the opportunity. Occasionally, you'll see where it's not quite clicking with the team. And then, whatever the talk is at halftime, the team often makes a shift or correction. Good coaches can motivate their players, give the right strategy, and stir them up. They might say, "Now, remember we went over this while we were practicing, but you're not quite hitting that mark; this is where you're missing it ... this strategy is what will fix that ... " That's what intermission is all about.

Can you hear Holy Spirit saying to our hearts, "Hey, let's stop right here! Let's let you rest and remember." (Or to say, "Re-member." Selah.) "Now, you know what the plan is. You know what I'm working toward." As Paul wrote in Philippians 1:6, "Being confident of this very thing, that He who has begun a good work in you will complete it until the day of Jesus Christ." So, the Holy Spirit is laying this out. God will complete His good work. His aim is clear. You know what was foreordained, but this is where you're missing the mark as far as pursuing the goal. Here's a strategy to give you some course corrections. That's what rest (intermission) can provide.

After considering these thoughts, you learn first to seek God's plan. I love this! He said, "You will find rest." What happens if one seeks? You will find it! Not that rest just finds you. But if you seek, you will find it. What should we have done with our time this year? We should have sought the Lord diligently. We should say, "Lord, what corrections, if any, do I need to make personally? What are they?" And then, apply them as He reveals them! Act on that. His correction is without condemnation. His correction is not rejection. It is called learning! If we just ask for the sake of asking with no intent to apply, that's called wasting time! You already have decided what you're going to do anyway. But, if you genuinely seek His strategy, you will find your intermission and rest with His instructions. They will be something practical for your soul.

Jesus said his yoke is easy! The original word here for *easy* has several words that come forth as synonyms in English. It indicates that it's useful, better, and easy; it is loaded with goodness, graciousness, and kindness. I say, "Amen!" So be it! Because a dose of kindness, graciousness, and goodness should be normal for a believer connected to Love Eternal! Goodness. Graciousness. Kindness. Come on! When Love is revealed, the sixteen characteristics of love are found in 1 Corinthians 13. In the text, the number two quality is kindness (v. 4). Love is kind. But the number one characteristic of love, and the first thing listed (law of first use) is that love is long-spirited or long-suffering. Scripture tells us that "charity [love] suffers long" (v. 4). That is love's number one quality.

The yoke is easy partly because longsuffering and kindness are designed to work **together**. For example, when someone passes through a difficult moment, we say, "I love you!" We attempt to show kindness and patience. Generally, we tell someone else what is common to humanity, whether meaning it or not. That's the kindness component. Right? But what about the long-suffering aspect? Let's assess the situation. We might say, "Oh, brother (or sister), I love you." But then, if they express wrongly or have the slightest fault or flaw in their behavior, you are suddenly no longer sure whether you love them. Why is that? Because, in the natural, so-called love (meaning the *feeling*) can be fake, flaky, or flimsy when you come out of the soul realm, untouched by the Holy Ghost. It can be a real mess.

Thankfully, love was so important that God did not leave it to us to define what it is! God defines for us what love is. First, he says, "Love is longsuffering" (v. 4). What is he telling us? God is love; therefore, God is longsuffering. An example of this in the scriptures is found in 2 Peter 3:9: "The Lord is not slack concerning his promise, as some men count slackness; but is longsuffering to us-ward, not willing that any should perish, but that all should come to repentance." Father God has been and continues to be gracious, kind, and long-suffering. He is our pattern.

Here's my point. Jesus offered an easy yoke. He also said "for my burden is light" (Mat. 11:30). His yoke and burden are interconnected. The word *burden,* in this instance, is defined as the task or service you are commissioned to execute. It is the bill of lading, the invoice you carry as the freighter or the vessel of the Lord. Wherever there's cargo, there's an invoice. The life of Christ is the cargo that you carry. Hallelujah. He's the cargo. There's an invoice. He said it is light—so light the wind can push it. Did you catch that? The wind, not human effort, drives it. It is not human ability apart from the touch of God that will get this moving!

This compares to holy men of God writing the Scriptures. The prophets (with some scribes and kings) primarily wrote the Old Testament. The apostles recorded the Scriptures comprising the New Testament. Therefore, we are built upon the foundation of the apostles and prophets. They were blown along (breathed, inspired), as it were, by the Holy Ghost in their writing. It wasn't them surmising and speculating some things and writing. The Holy Ghost was leading and directing them.

Jesus is telling them (and us) that when the burden is light and the yoke easy, the Holy Ghost is the engine, the power behind this. And so, in taking his yoke, we said that the encounter begins because of the invitation of Jesus. The rest that is given leads to refreshing because one receives by faith the invitation—Jesus becomes our spiritual oasis.

There's a yoke that the Lord Jesus gives us that replaces all and every other yoke we have borne (that is: allowed, tolerated, stomached, or accepted from the past). His is a learning yoke, and this yoke provides a ***discovered*** rest. In it, we discover that "Come unto me and I will give you rest," the Savior's perfect yoke, is more than solely an evangelistic message. <u>It is our instruction for the next portion of the journey.</u>

> That deep, soulish kind of rest is found in knowing that I am simply being obedient to the God who is bearing the burden. And because that's the case, the burden is never bearing down on me.
> — Craig Lounsbrough

CHAPTER TWO

FRUIT PRODUCERS

So God created man in his own image, in the image
of God created he him; male and female created he
them. And God blessed them, and God said unto
them, BE FRUITFUL, multiply, and replenish the
earth, and subdue it: and have dominion over the
fish of the sea, and over the fowl of the air, and over
every living thing that moveth upon the earth.
Genesis 1:27–28

Fruitfulness was always God's desire and is entirely dependent upon remaining in the Savior's perfect yoke. Remember our ending from the last chapter? Coming unto Him is His invitation and our instruction for the next portion of the journey! No one can pursue God except that God first pursued them. We love because He first loved us. Jesus gave several keys when He said in John 15:16, "You have not chosen me, but I have chosen you."

In decades past when I first attended Deliverance Temple in Jacksonville, North Carolina, we sang a song that spoke of our determination to journey with God. The lyrics are, "I have decided to follow Jesus. I have decided to follow Jesus. I have decided to follow Jesus; no turning back, no turning back."

When originally inspired, the song held a much different meaning than has developed over the decades of the modern church. Although the writer of the lyrics and the melody are listed as anonymous for the purposes of citation, we do know some of the song's history. In the middle of the 19th century, a tribal man converted to Christianity through the efforts of an American missionary. He is said to have recited verses from John 12 as he and his family were killed because of their faith. Hearing the story, the martyr's words were later turned into a hymn by an Indian missionary and became the song we know today. Even facing death, the believer responded to God in faith **because God first loved him**.

As I have matured in understanding, I have discovered that the modern expression of the song generally carries the tone that we are the instigators of the action. While a willing heart is essential, the meaning conveyed in this context is no longer completely accurate. It's impossible to decide of solely our own volition to follow Jesus.

Jesus said, "You don't come to the Father except the Father draws you to Himself." The Father comes to you and *gives you the invitation*. It is the same as Jesus inviting people to receive His yoke and burden. You may say, "Well, my struggles led me there." Ah! But the Father was still involved in the setup that led you to the moment. A. W. Tozer called this ***prevenient grace***[3].

Here's the concept: No one can pursue God except God first pursued them. That is a statement of truth. We know that. When you look at this idea of Him choosing us, not us choosing Him, we obtain better light on the subject. The timing of that is a set time; in Hebrew, it is called a ***moed:*** an appointed time, place, or meeting[4]. Appointed moments are divine interventions and require a response. It was always the Lord choosing us before we accepted that assignment or invitation. Our contribution demonstrates agreement with His choice.

I know brothers who have argued over the assignments of others. One of the questions goes like this: "Why do you get to be an apostle, and I'm just an evangelist?" Questions like this show that we often think in terms of pecking orders. We build stuff in our heads and make it stackable. Ministry assignments should never be viewed vertically; they should be horizontal relationships. You can see this when you study The Tabernacle of Moses. The rods and the poles connecting the boards weren't vertical; they were horizontal. And then, there was a central one across the full length of all the boards.

The central rod represents Christ. No other person can touch every board, but He does. Even the most mature ministers do not have the capacity to touch everyone. We do not need to get hung up on which ministry expression is the most important. God has a role for all of his Body to serve and fulfill. There is no place for competition or egos in serving God.

Let me give you an example of the ridiculousness of such conversations. One brother was introduced as an apostle **to the nations.** Everyone roared with appreciation for his ministry. The next speaker was introduced as an apostle **to the region.** What do you think happened? Once the speaker (the apostle to the region) stood behind the podium, he declared: "Well, bless God, I'm as much an apostle to the nations as he is!"

It was not very encouraging listening to this as a young minister. This was puzzling at first. I soon realized personal insecurities and pride run deep, even in mature ministers. It hadn't been completely flushed from their souls. This is not the way to conduct kingdom business. It is God that chooses our level of influence in His business. As Jesus said, "You didn't choose me, but I have chosen you." I'm making a point that we must remain passionately connected to Christ, not cool, cold, unenthusiastic, and certainly not competitive or envious.

Generally, we are blessed beyond measure when we begin ministry. We're going to take on the world with the good news of The Savior. We are full of zeal for Christ and easily enthusiastic about what God has asked us to do, and that's the only way to draw anyone else. Our callings and service should remain joyful as we rely on grace to help us. But over time, we often allow that to cool or grow stale.

I am reminded of a particular TV commercial advertising New Country Cornflakes. The singers sang unenthusiastically and deadpan. Do any of you remember that commercial?

That's not the way to begin a ministry. Those people looked twice dead and plucked up by the roots. But they're supposed to be convincing you that you need to have the cornflakes. I don't think so!

As a bonus note, that's why you always place smiling people as church greeters. Your greeters should never have a negative disposition about the ministry. No, you want somebody positive. They will greet guests with, "Wonderful to see you! This is a great place! Welcome!" Those greeters could have four or five teeth missing in the front, but it doesn't matter as long as they're smiling and loving the people. People should know you are happy they came. Let them know that they have found a loving, encouraging family who is inviting them to share life together.

Let's talk about that too—sharing life together. What does your enthusiasm as a leader do for people? Jesus did not say, as we go back to our original scripture, "Come unto me, and I'm going to make you worse than before." No! He said, "My yoke is easy, and My burden is light." That's an encouraging message, especially if you're honest enough to admit you're carrying a load. Sometimes we're too spiritual to admit difficulty. How are you doing, brother? Oh, I'm blessed and highly favored! That statement is true. But how do you reconcile that when you know, you spent the whole night in anger? The entire day before murmuring and complaining? Just in case you have forgotten, we are disobedient to the Word of God when we choose to behave that way. It doesn't mean that you're not blessed and highly favored. It means you're not living like you're blessed

and highly favored. There is an inconsistency that needs recti-
fying. And maybe, this was an opportunity to say, "Hey man,
I'm struggling a little bit!" The opportunity is present to invite
them to pray for you.

You know, it's shocking to observe the many little things
that begin to cool our spiritual temperature. It gradually happens until one day, you wake up and ask, "Where did my enthusiasm go? What happened?" Once a person walks with God
long enough, they will have at least one experience like that.
Yes, you will be left wondering. By remaining connected to
Christ, you will at least be able to get fired up again. Disconnected, you're only going to cool off and harden. Do you remember what the Lord said to the church at Ephesus? "Nevertheless I have this against you, that you have left your first love"
(Rev. 2:4; NKJV). In paraphrasing the context, He essentially
said, "You must change your mind, repent, and move forward."
Change your mind about how you're thinking and behaving,
and reconnect to the thing that's first. Jesus told them to keep
the first things first.

This is exactly the opposite of Adam. He disconnected and
remained that way for four millennia. Adam didn't remain
fixed on his Father. Look at what it produced. Paul, writing
on this in 1 Corinthians 6:17, said, "But he that is joined to
the Lord." Joined means to cleave, glued together. It's the same
concept that Jesus used in Matthew when he spoke about a
man leaving and cleaving. He cleaves to his wife. They become
glued together. We become one spirit when we are joined to
Christ.

Paul spoke even more about this during his sermon from Mars Hill. He said, "For in him we live, and move, and have our being; as certain also of your own poets have said, for we are also his offspring" (Acts 17:28). I wanted to know which poet said that. I searched and discovered who said it. The philosopher who was credited with that was Aratus, (flourished c. 315–c. 245 BC, Macedonia), Greek poet of Soli in Cilicia, in the poem he wrote called *Phaenomena*[5].

It is likely that Paul, being highly educated, was aware of this poem and poet Aratus lived about 300 years before him. He would be aware of things like this with the extensive studies he completed. Possibly, Aratus' discovery was a blind squirrel finding the acorn. Perhaps without consciously knowing it, the poet spoke the truth by saying our existence is in Him (God).

As Romans 1:20 says, those things in the visible creation teach us about the invisible things that can't be seen. I wish I could get into that a little deeper, but let's continue with this because we want to finish up strong about our subject of *being yoked* and *The Savior's Perfect Yoke*. Everything is tied to staying yoked in His perfect yoke because you are destined to produce more fruit and fruit that remains.

And, as we live in him, the allegory of union life with Christ is in the early part of John 15. Note that I'm going with The Passion Translation (TPT) for this *conversation* (with the understanding that it is a paraphrase not a literal translation):

I am a true sprouting vine, and the farmer who tends to the vine is my Father. He cares for the

branches connected to me by lifting and prop-
ping up the fruitless branches and pruning every fruitful branch to yield a greater harvest.
The words I have spoken over you have already
cleansed you. So you must remain in life-union
with me. For I remain in life-union with you.
For as a branch severed from the vine will not
bear fruit, so your life will be fruitless unless
you live your life intimately joined to me.
(John 15: 1 – 4, TPT)

Anytime you speak of this kind of union, one must pay attention to the construction of the Greek word it derives from.
We will get into that further in chapter four when we discuss
the prefix *syn-*. We find these unions expressed in the terms *synergy* and *synergistic relationships*, joinings that produce energy.
For now, union life is best described as united with the Christ-
life, utilizing association, companionship, completeness, and
process.

We are complete in him by nature. This life burgeons in
the New Testament, together with Christ, in union with Him.
It is used in seventeen different expressions by Paul, declaring
that this is the strength of our union in Christ. Seventeen is the
biblical number for total victory. A victorious life stands upon
the foundation of being in Christ.

Augustus H. Strong describes the union life in Christ this
way: It is an organic union, a vital union, a spiritual union, an
indescribable union, and an inscrutable union[6]. Each descrip-

tion gives synonyms of something natural and alive. The things we call supernatural should be natural for the sons of God. They should be our daily experiences. I have identified the kind of fruit that we desire to produce.

When you look at *vital*, it means *energetic and vibrant*. Hallelujah! You will have a real enthusiasm for this life. Glory to God! This is essential when talking to others about it. It's like light rays beaming out of you so much that someone would have to put on a veil. *Spiritual* means it's *unworldly*. It's non-physical; it's transcendent. That means the life within us is indissoluble; it's *permanent, binding, and unbreakable*.

When life is viewed as *inscrutable*, it is *enigmatic or incomprehensible*. The mystery of the inscrutable relationship of things connected in a union has interested both scientists and scholars for centuries.

Most people have heard of Albert Einstein. Einstein was a theoretical physicist. He was a thinker and would propose things that other physicists working in the laboratory would prove out. Einstein did not believe two particles could remain connected to each other over great distances; doing so, he said, would require them to communicate faster than the speed of light, something he felt had been previously shown to be impossible.

Through the years, however, other physicists have proven Einstein was incorrect about the inscrutable relationship of things connected in a union. In ground-breaking scientific experiments, the question was posed if a piece of a molecule breaks off from the source and travels into another portion of the universe, would activity in the molecule register in the source? Today, experimental work leaves no doubt that quantum entanglement is real. We now know this commonly as Quantum Physics.

Now, let's bring this into Kingdom thinking because the visible and invisible should reveal the truth to us. Let's look at the scripture on this concept of Christ-life union. Jesus spoke incredible things when separating sheep and goat nations. The difference between the two was their response to practical Kingdom realities. Sheep nations fed the Lord when He was hungry. Goat nations didn't! Within the context of the scripture, was He, The Lord, here and hungry? He also spoke about being thirsty, sick, and in prison. In both cases, Jesus tells us that our response to the least of His people was our response to Him. Like a piece of bread broken from the Bread of Life and shared, we are a piece of Him released on this earth while He remains in the heavens.

When Jesus said that what is done to His brethren is done to Him, it was a powerful statement. This thing is bigger than cause and effect. Look at it this way: when you came out of the Heavenly Father as a spirit, he got your biological parents together so you could have a body. It was more than a good idea; it was a God idea! God is Spirit, and we are like the particle in the experiment as a spirit being that broke away by design from the source. We are on this earth, and whatever is happening to one of us affects all of us. We must conclude that our actions on earth affect our Lord Jesus Christ. Sheep nations conduct themselves properly, whereas goat nations do not. We're going to realize how deeply connected we are to one another—but <u>not</u> in the way new-age universalists like to depict. It is more powerful than we thought.

But, back to our principal discussion. God yoked Himself to Israel in the Old Testament. They did not understand this depth, nor did they comprehend the art of communion with God. In Psalm 80:8, God said, "I took you out of Egypt, and you were like a tender plant. And then I planted you in the land, and you were my vineyard." He also said, "I evicted the other nations and put you there" (my paraphrase). He wanted them to remain connected with Him. But here's the deal: They disconnected themselves by their disobedience and became unfruitful.

Consequently, the fence that usually protects the vineyard was broken down by trespassers. They compared it to beasts breaking over the walls to ravage the vineyard. The cry in Psalm 80 asked the Lord to connect them again because fruit production stops when people are disconnected from their source.

God has made our identity clear to us, but it's up to us to yield to that. He will not force us to yield to or obey His commandments. A cry for a deeper connection should be coming from the church. Those who have an understanding should deeply connect.

Lord, may we study as the Word tells us. We're to learn from the things that happened, realizing that the ends of the ages have come upon us. Let us learn, Lord, and not repeat history by being disconnected. Let us learn from Adam. What happened to him when he made his decision? He chose misinformation rather than the revelation from his Father's heart. We must learn from what his life became and how it affected every other life on the planet. We learned that disconnection only produces death. Let us learn that the body is a visual of that. When the spirit of man disconnects from the physical, that is biological death. We must remain in the Savior's perfect yoke.

When Isaiah spoke to Israel (see in context in Isaiah 5:1–7), He declared they had become an unproductive vineyard. Think about what they could have done. Yes, think of all the advantages they had, including the prophets and the covenants. But because of disobedience, they became unfruitful. And so, our prayer should be, "God, may we become aware of our need to accept your invitation afresh." When He said, "Come unto me," it doesn't matter if one is late in life or up in years. Jesus will give you the kind of yoke you're supposed to bear as a son of God. It is easily worn and a burden to bear on this side.

This is not solely a new birth invitation; it's an invitation to be continually refreshed. The Heavenly Father desires us to get enthusiastic about our assignment and follow through with it!

Fruit-bearing involves cross-bearing. There are not two Christs—an easygoing one for easygoing Christians, and a suffering, toiling one for exceptional believers. There is only one Christ. Are you willing to abide in Him and thus to bear much fruit?
— Hudson Taylor

CHAPTER THREE

ESSENTIALS TO FRUITFULNESS

If ye abide in me, and my words abide in you, ye
shall ask what ye will, and it shall be done unto you.
Herein is my Father glorified, that ye bear much fruit;
so shall ye be my disciples. As the Father hath loved
me, so have I loved you: continue ye in my love.
John 15:7–8

In these next two chapters, there are five things that I want
to bring forward. Our focus in this text has been on remaining yoked to the Savior's perfect yoke. That will involve vision casting or stating some goals. As we go through life's journey, we should write down thoughts that the Holy Spirit has placed in our hearts.

We would do well to begin this exercise in the last two months of every year as we head into each new year. Frequently, we make new year's resolutions only to find that they are no longer intact by the end of February. One year I said, "I'm going to lose fifteen pounds, and I lost them. But then they found me again. Yes, I let them go, but they said, "No! We like you!" What is my point? We make resolutions with good intent to follow through and sometimes even make some strides toward them. Still, if the Holy Spirit isn't the one energizing us, these commitments will always be broken.

When God gives the vision, the related goals are not like resolutions. In John 15, Jesus said, "I am the true vine. And my father is the husbandman" (v. 1). He's the farmer that dresses the vines. "Every branch in me that beareth not fruit is removed" (v. 2). This fruitfulness would be connected to us as we minister to those within our sphere of influence.

So, you can look at it this way—fruit-bearing centers around the fruit of the Spirit. The fruit of the Spirit flows over into the body. This is true whether the spirit is renewed in Christ or unredeemed. **The state of a person's spirit dictates the fruit it produces.**

An erroneous teaching circulating distinguishes between sins of the flesh and sins of the spirit. The premise is that one would not affect the other, and it discounts the importance of the human body. They believe and teach sins of the flesh will only affect your flesh, but sins of the spirit affect your relationship with God. The error of that teaching is that whether committed by the spirit or flesh, sin's payoff is death.

These teachings derived from Gnosticism because of what they taught about man's flesh. They taught that the flesh is unimportant and of no value to God. I will tell you now; God placed importance on the spirit, the soul, and the body. He did not divide them to eliminate any particular one, and He did not minimize one at the expense of the other. A whole person is made of spirit, soul, and body. When people expire physically, this alone gives added importance to the resurrection. The resurrection reality provides several things. God raised our spirit out of sins and trespasses into life. We are currently walking through the transforming and renewing of our minds to rid us of carnality. That's a second resurrection. And, in the end, resurrection affects our bodies. We receive a glorified body.

If someone should lay this body aside for a short season, the time comes when it's picked up again. That's the resurrection! It's not raised in the humiliation it died in but in glory. A true metamorphosis occurs. A new form emerges because God places equal importance on all three—spirit, soul, and body. And so, when that discussion presents itself (distinguishing between sins of the flesh and sins of the spirit), you will know where the narrative began. It's nothing but a conversation that has its roots in the flesh.

Be careful with that one! The wages of sin are always horrible. God intends that we would bear fruit and not the fruit of death. Jesus said, "Every branch in me that beareth not fruit, he taketh away" (v. 2).

I understand this concept well. I worked in tobacco growing up in North Carolina. There was a point in the growing process when you would have to "suckle the tobacco." You would have little leaves growing between the stalk and the larger leaf that would rob the larger leaf of life. It was necessary to destroy the suckles to get your best production, so we removed them.

Next, the tops of the tobacco plants had to be broken off. They also prevented the greatest productivity in the plant. Both these examples are metaphors for connected lives (like those tops) which are not bearing fruit. So, what is the remedy? Pruning away the dead things for life to flourish. We must be willing to remove every kind of ministry (and life) expression that is not bearing fruit.

Let's look at a Bible example in Luke 13:8–9. There was a vineyard owner who identified an unfruitful tree. The gardener said to the owner, "Let's let it alone this year, and I will dig about it and dung it: and if it bears fruit, great: and if not, then after that, we will cut it down" (paraphrased). Does that sound familiar? That is great for the things that bloom again and respond to proper attention. But what about all the things we have already been holding on to for years of unfruitfulness? What would happen if we just went ahead and dealt with them? If anything on our branches prevents us from bearing fruit, remove it without prejudice.

Let me share a short story with you. I took a small break from pastoring a church full-time a few years ago. I had pastored for twenty years, and that was a good thing. It was the direction that I sensed from the Lord at the time. However, I didn't break completely away from ministry. I didn't stop the pastoral ministry because I was upset or bitter against anyone. It was a season for refocusing on the various assignments the Lord had given me. Also, I took Jesus' instructions not to live in anger and bitterness of heart. Yes, some negative things had happened, but I didn't allow them to get into my heart. I dealt with them through the help of the Holy Spirit.

In the meantime, we stored the ministry equipment for future use, thinking we'll return to the pastoral ministry someday. Finally, a few years ago, I realized I might never return to that same expression of ministry after paying the storage fees for years. I had to face the question, "Why are you keeping this, especially if you are not returning to this?"

I shared this recently in one of our God's Kingdom Leaders' Summits, and as I did, the class became extremely quiet when I presented that question. I realized they were thinking about *their stuff*. We must ask ourselves, "Why are we keeping things from a previous season in life?" I suggest doing an inventory and preparing to dispense some things. How many of you have done that recently? For example, I know many of your closets are full. What things haven't you worn in two years? Remember that we are learning to release the old yoke and take the Savior's perfect yoke. His yoke is secure and plentiful. So, how about we identify them and release them to someone else? I am certain someone could benefit from our charity.

While we are releasing some extra out of our closets, let me be clear that I'm not talking about worn-out clothing with two or three holes. That needs to be in the trash, not the seed bin. I'm not talking about the suit you have worn thin and your backside is showing through. That's not what you give away. You should give other people things you like and enjoy using or receiving. If it is trash, you need to release it by throwing it away.

A covetous heart is the only thing that stops us from releasing our abundance. The spirit of covetousness will have us holding stuff to simply possess it. Not me. I will not allow that to rule my heart or our lives. Besides, if you never sow any seed, there will be no opportunity for harvest.

Everything I'm speaking about is a setup for fruit-bearing. Every branch connected to Christ should bear fruit. If so, you're in good condition. When you're not bearing fruit, the other condition carries the expectation of becoming a castaway. It's like a tree in the yard that's holding dead limbs. How long are you going to let them hang there? You can let them hang there, fall on their own, or take them away.

Jesus said, even when you're bearing fruit, he will purge you. Did you know that the verb used in Jesus' statement from John 15:2 is a form of the word *catharsis*, which means to prune, purge, or cleanse? Now I realize that some of you may have been around or grown up in a church where they "purged the brethren." If you have or did, then I'm sorry you had that experience. If you've never been in a purging service, you missed something! It was so horrible you wouldn't ever want to be in another. I remember a few times (not at my home church but in other places) I would visit those churches with some of my early mentors. They instructed me not to be surprised by the things I might see. Possibly, there could be a purging service. I had no clue what a purging service was. When I left there, I was no longer ignorant. I equally knew that was not for Steve! So just in case you have had that experience, that is definitely not what we are talking about here! And neither was Jesus.

We are speaking of biblical pruning or purging, pruning away anything that keeps us from growing in Christ. Jesus said if we bear fruit, he will purge us because we haven't yet fully bloomed and produced. He informed us that further trimming takes us to maximum production.

Let's go further with this thought. Jesus prunes us to bring forth *more* fruit, and that's my point. It isn't pruning or trimming just because He has the authority to do it. *More* indicates we haven't reached the maximum yet. Now come down to John 15. Jesus said, "Abide in Me. The branch cannot bear fruit except it abides in the vine" (v. 4; paraphrased). He was talking about staying yoked in the Savior's perfect yoke; no son of God can bear fruit except he abides in Jesus.

Then he said, "I am the Vine, and you are the branches" (v. 5). Abiding in Him is the best environment, the right environment to bear much fruit. Taking our discussion even further, the concept of "Christ in us" is the **right Seed**. If you get the right environment and the right seed yoked together, the two bring forth not just fruit **but much fruit**. Much fruit means you are abundantly producing. It is plentiful.

Now, any way you slice that, if you move through the progression, God intends that life without is an expression of the quality of life working within you. It should produce much because you have eternal life within you.

35

Theoretically, this is true. However, we still see lots of poverty. God wants to strip us of any vestiges of poverty remaining in our lives. Yet for decades, a large portion of the Body of Christ has rejected teaching from the Word on biblical prosperity. I have yet to understand the angry response to God's Word teaching on prosperity and victory. Really? Did we enjoy poverty in our churches? Did we think impoverished houses and neighborhoods signify God's blessings? Maybe, you are one of the fortunate ones that never experienced any of that. But I did.

People called them the "good old days." I never want to see them again. I never want to see corn cobs or the pages from the store catalog become toilet tissue again. After discovering real toilet tissue, you no longer want to return to the former days.

Let us return to God's original intent. He said, "Be fruitful, multiply, replenish, and subdue the earth." This mandate includes three stages of fruit-bearing. The fourth word, *subdue*, involves protecting and maintaining what has been produced.

This brings us to the root of why catharsis is necessary. Catharsis, pruning or purging away the old lifeless limbs, enables us to bring forth more fruit. And then, as you remain connected to Christ, you will grow stronger and healthier in the right environment, which is the will of God. Also, by keeping the right seed in you, which is the Word of God, you will be fruitful. Remember, the Word of God is an incorruptible seed. Hallelujah!

Our potential is limitless when we remain in the right environment with the right seed. It is the *much fruit mandate* of

Jesus. And so, as he deals with this, he reminds them that you can do nothing without me. We must remember that as well. I would repeat that daily many years ago. "I can do nothing without him." Even a better heart attitude is that I don't want to do anything without Him.

Consider John 15:8: "Herein is my Father glorified that you bear much fruit." God is glorified when we are the most productive. This statement meant that the original dominion mandate was still in effect. Jesus said The Father was glorified when He finished His assignment on earth. So, based upon Jesus' testimony, He bore much fruit.

In John 15:16, Jesus made another most powerful statement: "Ye have not chosen me, but I have chosen you and ordained you." In each statement, He's reminding the disciples of the importance of staying yoked to Him, abiding in the Savior's perfect yoke. It isn't the quantity but the quality you put into a life that bears much fruit.

For instance, people make a lot out of modern ordinations. Are they biblical? Truthfully, the term is different. When we say ordination, a certificate or license is presented to the candidate recognized by men. But in truth, real ordination is something that God does, not men. Can I set the record straight? Again, this is a series for maturing ones, for leaders. To be godly leaders, we must know the Word and live by it. God said to Jeremiah, "Before I formed you in the womb I knew you; Before you were born I sanctified you; I ordained you a prophet to the nations" (Jeremiah 1:4 NKJV). So we see that **God ordained him**. So, *ordination is a God thing*. Ordination means that

God sets the horizon in advance before he ever forms the vessel that will move toward that horizon.

At some point, we wake up to what God has ordained. Like Jeremiah, **we come into a knowledge of what is already true.** Others may ask you about your ordination just as men asked Jesus in Mark 11:28 (NKJV), "By what authority are You doing these things? And who gave You this authority to do these things?" In modern language, they're asking him, "Who authorized you to do what you do?" Or, "What organization ordained you?" Or perhaps, "Who gave you your license to preach?" When I was growing up in North Carolina, it might have been, "Do you have a fellowship card?"

A license is different from an ordination. A license is what organizations confer as they officially recognize that you're called and set apart by someone other than yourself. It's an outward acknowledgment that you haven't gone to the water and baptized yourself as an apostle (or other titles) with no witnesses!

That might seem strange or funny to think of, but it happens. It is so common that a movie was written in jest about it and the hypocrisy of those who launch of their own ordaining. *The Apostle* is a 1997 American drama film written and directed by Robert Duvall. In the movie, The Apostle Euliss F. "Sonny" Dewey (played by Duvall) is portrayed as a lively preacher. Here is the movie's premise:

His wife Jessie has begun an adulterous relationship with a youth minister named Horace. She refuses Sonny's desire to reconcile, although she assures him that she will not interfere with his right to see his children. She has also conspired to use their church's bylaws to have him removed from power. Sonny asks God what to do but receives no answer. Much of the congregation sides with Jessie in this dispute. Sonny, however, refuses to start a new church, insisting that the one which forced him out was "his" church. At his child's Little League game, Sonny, in an emotional and drunken fit, attacks Horace with a bat and puts him into a coma; Horace later dies.

A fleeing Sonny ditches his car in a river and gets rid of all identifying information. After destroying all evidence of his past, Sonny re-baptizes himself and anoints himself as "The Apostle E. F." He leaves Texas and ends up in the bayous of Louisiana, where he persuades a retired minister ... to help him start a new church. He works various odd jobs and uses the money to build the church and to buy time to preach on a local radio station.

The police show up in the middle of an evening service but allow Sonny to finish it while they wait outside. In the poignant finale, Sonny delivers an impassioned sermon before telling his flock that he has to go. He leaves with the officers and after due process is imprisoned. The movie ends in the final scenes with Sonny [now part of a prison work crew] preaching to the inmates as they work along the side of a highway.

My reason for including that fictional account is that entertainment mimics real events and culture. The church and the world are both full of self-appointed, self-titled individuals. We must learn and do better. Scripture is clear that this is not the biblical pattern. What is the biblical pattern? God had ordained Jesus' purpose in the earth. And God ordained the steps of each apostle. Father God commissioned Jesus, and Jesus commissioned the twelve apostles. There is always someone in greater Kingdom authority that does the commissioning. In Acts 13, the Holy Ghost released Barnabas and Saul to act officially as the representative of Christ. They were commissioned and *released to do the work* God ordained for them to do.

So, there's a major difference between ordination and commissioning. God ordained me; however, the leadership at Deliverance Temple commissioned me. Jesus was telling the apostles, "I'm commissioning you next." The Father commissioned me first. They were free to go and carry out their assignments. The expectation was that the apostles would bring forth fruit that would remain. They needed to stay connected to Jesus. He also gave them a wonderful promise. The Heavenly Father would grant their desires when they prayed in Jesus' name.

When you go as a Kingdom ambassador, you must bring forth fruit that remains. Jesus told them to remain connected without getting cool or lukewarm in the heart. You don't have to become conceited because you're chosen. You're commissioned without any confusion. You're copious, producing fruit without covetousness. Jesus told them to remain close—intimate. The consistency in your communion will keep you yoked to Jesus.

> Love is a fruit in season at all times and
> within reach of every hand.
> — Mother Teresa

CHAPTER FOUR

THE WORK

As they ministered to the Lord and fasted, the Holy Ghost said, 'Separate me Barnabas and Saul for the work where unto I have called them.' And when they had fasted and prayed and laid hands on them, they sent them away.
Acts 13:2–3

The Holy Ghost yoked Barnabas and Saul together, and the other brethren commissioned them to the work. I want to paint a picture to give us an understanding of this concept. We're introduced to this thought in Acts 13. They (Barnabas and Saul) became yokefellows. When John Mark was added to the team, he served the apostles as an under-oarsman. This means that he was their helper and rendered service with his hands.

In Acts 13:13, however, we see that John Mark left the team abruptly. At that moment, Mark needed further character development. Later in 2 Timothy 4:11, we'll see that John Mark matures to where he can once again be counted on as a faithful servant of God, profitable to Paul for the ministry.

For now, let's look at the assignment and why it's essential to be re-energized. The Lord knows we need revitalization, so He brings us to seasons of rest or intermission. Freshness is essential to doing the work. That will give us an advantage in our assignments.

So, it is Holy Spirit who energizes us in the assignment. He gives grace-filled energy. One of the ways to help prolong life is to lean into the Holy Spirit's energy and learn to build *synergistic relationships* with support leaders. Let's unravel that thought. We have the word energy in *synergistic (adj.)* or *synergy (n.)*, plus the Greek prefix *syn*. When "syn-" comes before the word, it speaks to union life, joined together, or yoked with the primary word. There's a union with the existing energy. The Holy Spirit is the one that gives us the energy of God.

When you birth a new work, you especially need that energy. Here is one example. Pastors Jon and April Oxendine started a brand-new work (Reformation Church) in Southern Pines, North Carolina. The work is several years old now at the time of this publishing, but initially, most of the work depended heavily upon the Holy Spirit's energy *in them*. Pastors of new works will often do almost everything at first. Yes, they will minister the Word of God, pastor the sheep, and do whatever needs to be done. They will be the janitors until others are trained to help. They will be their own under-rowers by doing everyday practical tasks and completing administrative responsibilities. But, like Pastor Jon and Pastor April and many others, their leading by example will help synergistic relationships to develop. It is vital to the work that they pattern and remain fixed on what God shows them is the work *they* have been ordained to and *how they are to do it.* Then, you will reproduce that vision.

The key is to hear from God, know what you have been directed to do, and the way He told you to do it; express that desire and present that, or we should say, present *Him.* As He is rightly represented, relationships will grow, and destiny helpers will come alongside in the right synergy to contribute rightly to the work! Every work must be led by the Holy Spirit, and every leader must be the example of following the Holy Spirit and not their own agendas. This is how we set the standard for *what God has joined.* This is how others learn *how to help that specific work.*

In retrospect, I didn't do that very well when I was a much younger man. That hurt everyone, including me! People began to take liberties that they shouldn't be taking. A great conflict erupted because of unclear communication in the beginning. Still today, I am remodeling those early examples in my long-term relationships, correcting the course when people begin or continue to take liberties that they shouldn't. This includes causing conflict by inserting their own agendas rather than what the Holy Spirit has defined as the work. *Michelle and I are committed to and actively cultivating being properly yoked in a culture of synergistic honor.* It's the decision that is the highest and best for The Kingdom, and it is also what is best and most healthy for us and all who are connected by God with us. It is a priority in our God's Kingdom Leaders' Summits and in our fellowship with all those God has joined with this ministry.

Every leader should lay hold of this tightly: When God trusts *you* with an assignment, you shouldn't just let anyone and everyone do whatever they think is best in whatever manner they desire to do so. Sure, you need help, but receiving just any idea or contribution will not prove to be helpful in the longer term. If it's not God's directive, it will lead to destruction. And the directives for the work He has assigned to you to complete will come through Holy Spirit *to you.*

I like to share how my wife Michelle's pastors for several decades, Brother Keith and Mrs. Phyllis Moore, taught her this (which they have also shared in their public broadcasts). Having started an international travel ministry, an international fellowship of ministers, and two strong churches by Holy Spirit's leadership, Brother Moore says, "I don't do what I want to do; why would I do what you want me to do?" You know, I believe this is what is appropriate and a biblical response to those voices who want to criticize, assert opinions, or those who would desire to take liberties or vary from the vision directives of the ministry while volunteering! He has shared that they are committed to doing *what God said to do*, not acting on their own personal desires, and neither are they moved by the desires, directions, or pressures asserted from others. That's how to operate in grace-filled energy! We observe that they have continued to be fruitful and multiply because of their synergy and clear understanding of the grace that is engaged when being led by Holy Spirit.

The apostles were master builders in God's work. Paul used the word architect to describe this. The architect had the blueprints. If you have the blueprints, you have the plans of how things should go. The foundation of this blueprint is Christ. Paul clearly stated that there was no other foundation. He cautioned others on how they built upon the foundation. One doesn't haphazardly tear down all in the name of building afresh. We must remove older concepts to plant and build the right ones. But it is never wise to go in and blow everything up with or without proper assessment. It is unwise to do that because you will also destroy the people.

We are not in the business of destroying people. We want to remove, pluck up the concept, and replace anything that prevents them from maturing in Christ. That's a life-giving action. Paul had clear instructions for those who build further because none of us are the first ones building from Jesus. That honor was given to the first century servants of Christ. We are all now in the synergistic building stage. Many others have been added to the building process once you get beyond that first generation. And when others have been added, that creates synergy, which is much more powerful.

For example, the synergy that empowered this current move of God came from the Latter Rain Movement. I'm speaking of the time between 1947 to 1955. Many of those servants of

God didn't live very long. Some of the more prominent ones died early. Why? When you think about the great anointing in these vessels, why didn't it give them longevity? There is a powerful reason. Many of them did not master trusted synergistic relationships. They did just about every bit of the preaching, praying, and ministering to people. That wasn't the best thing to do. Are you hearing me here? Ultimately, each of us must trust someone. Here is the reason: If the Lord lingers in His physical return, each of us will go to meet him. This earth will be left with the work continuing. *The work will not halt until The Father's purposes are fully executed.*

We must be confident that our motive is to *build people*, not our own names. Yes, build people! We once thought building a nice building was the best work. I'm grateful for buildings. However, my purpose is to cause the Christ within you to spring up. If I don't accomplish that, I haven't done the work. Michelle and I have this in common. We came to be "as One among you who serves" (Luke 22:25–27). As more of us aim for this same assignment, the work will be accomplished with the excellency of God.

Are you with me here? Paul and the team consumed great energy as they traveled in ministry. We read in Acts 14:21–22:

> And when they had preached the gospel to that city and had taught many, they returned again to Lystra, and to Iconium, and Antioch, confirming the souls of the disciples, and exhorting them to continue in the faith, and that we

through much tribulation enter into the Kingdom of God.

There are two operations of grace in these verses—the apostolic plants and waters. Once people are planted in the things of God, they must be watered (strengthened) to continue in the faith. Much of my teaching ministry through the years has been watering the saints.

Luke stated in Acts 14:23, "And when they had ordained them elders in every church and had prayed with fasting, they commended them to the Lord, on whom they believed." We see that the apostles identified leaders developing in relatively young works. They recognized a grace on some to be elders. They recognized others as deacons and other ministers of helps.

Listen, leaders, it's not about waiting twenty or thirty years until someone finally arrives. We must trust the mighty hand of God in the lives of others. Yes, we must trust the builder of the church—that's Jesus Christ. We must trust the agent he's working through—the Holy Spirit. And we must train and trust the younger ones to develop and confirm their function. We see clearly in scripture that the apostolic team confirmed leaders. They prayed with fasting and commended them to the Lord. We must do the same to those submitted under our leadership. Some things will only be learned by engaging in the work.

Now, I'm not telling any leader to be vulnerable to people's ambitions and fail to discern impure motives. We should always be aware of intents that are not good for the Kingdom of God. We must be fearless to do that. It is neither healthy nor godly to be fearful when we must be proactive in our decision-making.

Some years ago, I hit a very difficult season with some leaders. So, I turned them over to the Lord. But I should have turned them over to the Lord in the beginning. And then, I wouldn't have had to worry about them anyway. This action didn't absolve me of my leadership responsibilities.

By teaching the correct biblical pattern in these God's Kingdom Leaders' Summits (and the related series of studies and books), our prayer is that many who may have disqualified themselves or abandoned the work previously (not with us necessarily, but wherever and however they have done so) will avail themselves of this fresh opportunity (like John Mark did with Paul) to redeem the relationships and step back into the Savior's perfect yoke again. Like David, John Mark, Peter, and so many others, God is speaking to many today that it is not too late or too far gone for you to return again to God's best for your life. He still beckons you to "Come unto me!" In God's great grace-filled synergy, you can become of great value to those God intended you to serve alongside. Luke wrote in Acts 14:24–26 (emphasis added):

> And after they had passed throughout Pisidia, they came to Pamphylia. And when they had preached the word in Perga, they went down into Attalia: And then sailed to Antioch, from

whence they had been recommended to the grace of God for *the work* which they fulfilled.

The apostolic team is constantly moving. Movement is the character of the apostolic paradigm. Their work is not a weekend endeavor in which one preaches for two or three days and returns home. The trip wasn't a glorious vacation either. Do you realize all that happened on this first trip? After returning home, Paul could say, "Well, they stoned me, but I didn't remain dead." He's informing us that there's a cost to do the work. Even after being stoned, the team committed to additional follow-up. Much was at stake in these actions. That was to safeguard the kingdom's pollination of each work that was being planted.

I've been calling for more pollinators. I'm very thankful for all the stationary ministries (pastors, elders, deacons, deaconess). Still, we need the pollinators (apostles, prophets, evangelists) to join them to strengthen the works. There aren't that many today because the money is tighter, or some think it is. They refuse to be pollinators anymore. And many churches refuse to invite pollinators anymore. We must remember that the Heavenly Father is our source. As we seek first the Kingdom and our Father's righteousness, we shouldn't be concerned about provision. As God said to Abram in a vision, "Fear not, Abram: I am thy shield, and thy exceeding great reward" (Genesis 15:1).

But what would happen to the earth if we didn't have pollinators? Do you realize life on earth would cease to be without the bees, the pollinators? Life in the kingdom will not be as effective as it can be if you don't have pollinators. Paul and Barnabas were pollinating after these works were planted. They would go back to pollinate them with more understanding of the kingdom. They continued confirming them, raising leaders, and building synergistic relationships. They were clear about these endeavors in the work of the Kingdom.

Their reason for doing this was that death was a real possibility at any time. They also knew Caesar and the Jews were not pleased with them as they preached the gospel. They understood the cost, and they weren't fearful and self-contained. The apostles refused to lock themselves into a small way of thinking. They were 100% given to the work of the Kingdom. Their building and synergistic mentality prevented works from dissolving, even if they transitioned from this earth. Their deaths were like seeds. Most works grew exponentially after the initial grace carriers returned to The Father. They may have left, but their anointing remained and multiplied in a corporate body.

The mentality in those days was for the next anointed person to step up! It's easy to understand if you think of it like a sports team. In sports, the coaches and the team know who is ready to move forward if a man goes down. This is because they constantly prepare the reserves to step up. At the professional level, there are certain positions that coaches will cover four deep! That's how God wants us to think in the kingdom of God. We should always build for continuance and expansion. There is a simple reason behind this. It is all about the Kingdom of God and not about maintaining our kingdoms. If any among us have been building with that mentality, they cannot build that way going forward. Look at what happens in Acts 15:36–38:

> And some days after Paul said unto Barnabas, "Let us go again and visit our brethren in every city where we have preached the Word of the Lord, and see how they do." And Barnabas determined to take with them John, whose surname was Mark. But Paul thought it not good to take him with them, who departed from them from Pamphylia and went not with them to the work.

Please note that Paul has become the primary voice in the relationship, or at least the most vocal. When first released, the Holy Ghost sent them as Barnabas and Saul. And now it appears that Paul is leading the team. What happened? Remember, the Holy Spirit was guiding and never became confused.

Barnabas and Saul had contention because of differing opinions about John Mark. Rather than staying yoked, they let it separate them. I realized Paul became the primary speaker because of the grace that was on him. Becoming the chief speaker doesn't make one in charge of the relationship. The Holy Spirit had already set the order. They should have mutually submitted to one another until an agreement was reached about Mark. Instead, it cost them. And equally, it would cost any of us who allow contentious opinions to rule decisions.

I've had calls from men in the past. It was clear their wives carried the grace for the work. They struggled because other men told them to take over. Yet, they didn't have the grace to do it in most cases. The wife had the primary grace for the work. As for Barnabas, the Holy Ghost called his name first. Someone might say, "Barnabas, Paul is an aggressive man. Take the leadership of this relationship back. Slow the train down!" **God wanted them launched into the work.** Whether Paul was led by the Holy Spirit or led by his mind is up for consideration. His desire to visit the brethren was legitimate and necessary. They were going there for a time of evaluation.

There are times churches will have me come in for that same purpose. As I contribute wise counsel to other ministers or churches with whom I have a relationship, I may ask, "How can I help you before going? Or is there something specific that's needed?" Other times, the Lord will simply say to me, "This is needed." What enables us to navigate through that relationship? There's a simple answer: We trust the integrity of each other's intentions.

And so Barnabas determined to take John Mark, but Paul thought it was not good to take him with them. Mark had departed from them from Pamphylia. Paul hadn't yet seen or recognized the needed development or maturity in Mark, whereas Barnabas believed he was ready.

A divine moment comes in a spiritual father's life when he recognizes that his son has matured beyond his early days of ministry. He is as capable as the father is of doing the work. He's not the same person that made early mistakes. Many times, fathers may not think their sons are ready. At some point, that opinion must change. Let me give you a supporting scripture:

> Now if Timotheus come, see that he may be with you without fear: for he worketh the work of the Lord, as I also do. Let no man therefore despise him: but conduct him forth in peace, that he may come unto me: for I look for him with the brethren. (1 Corinthians 16:10–11)

Paul had changed through the years. He elevated Timothy to the same level as himself. Timothy was doing the same work as Paul. He didn't see him as an apostolic trainee anymore. He wasn't patting him on the head and telling him, "Someday, you will get there!" Or "Someday, you'll be as deep as I am. You'll be deep enough to understand what I'm saying to you." That wasn't how Paul treated Timothy. He recognized great value in Him. While others may have built differently, Paul built to replace himself. Did you hear me? **There's work that must be done. We must prepare the saints to do the work of the ministry.**

Dr. Bill Hamon wrote a book several years ago focusing on the ministry of the saints. This *ministry of the saints* will be the greatest ministry that ever hit the planet. The apostles (sent out ones) and all of the five-fold ministry gifts help prepare the saints to do the work of the ministry. Using Paul's words from Colossians 2, we too agonize in labor to make sure the saints are maturing! **Think of how powerful the saints will be as**

they cooperate more and more with the Holy Ghost and move in total agreement with the Word of God. James says it this way:

> But be ye doers of the word, and not hearers only, deceiving your own selves. For if any be a hearer of the word and not a doer, he is like unto a man beholding his natural face in a glass: For he beholdeth himself, and goeth his way, and straightway forgetteth what manner of man he was. But whoso looketh into the perfect law of liberty, and continueth therein, he being not a forgetful hearer, but a doer of the work, this man shall be blessed in his deed. (James 1:22–25)

James is speaking to believers about doing the work! In the case of Barnabas and Paul, the work was planting and watering local churches. They wanted to make sure those churches grew strong by making regular visits. They labored to mature them for the work, to mature them as doers of the Word of God!

Now, there is something I haven't mentioned yet. Let's address the attitude some have about ministry. "Well, I'll make this trip if the honorarium is right." No! Come on! Yes, a worker is worth his wages, and the Word is the most valuable thing we can bring to another. But what did I tell you earlier? We must trust that God is our source. And if He says, "Go." I go! My practice is to listen to God's voice and obey. It is the only way to willingly remain in the Savior's perfect yoke. **We must get this right!** "For as many as are led by the Spirit of God, *they* are the sons of God" (Romans 8:14; emphasis added).

When God began to send me on assignments internationally, I realized that the condition of my body would be important upon my arrival. For instance, after a sixteen-hour non-stop flight to South Africa, I felt tired in several ways. We changed time zones seven times during that flight. It was more difficult to minister in that physical condition. I pressed through, and He sustained me. When I went to Malaysia, it was twenty-eight hours, mainly across the ocean. Again, it was very hard on the body, especially for a strong adult man six feet tall!

Eventually I said to the Lord, "You know I'll go any place you want me to go. But I have now realized my body's condition is also important once I land. My hosts would expect me to begin ministry shortly after my arrival. I didn't have the luxury of resting several days before ministry. So, I am asking you for provision for a seat upgrade." I finally decided to believe God to sit in the business class rather than the coach class. It is His assignment, after all. And He is not limited, except by our lack of faith. And I have had that and more for every trip since that request.

I am still talking about being led by the Spirit of God. I am still speaking of being called and equipped for the work! Because we often think small, we settle for less than God has for us. I had a friend that behaved like that (being poverty minded, thinking small) until he witnessed how much more refreshed and ready to minister I was as a result of the upgrade. He was all in for it then and wanted to trade seats with me on the return trip. Of course, smiling, I said, "No."

It would be unfair of me to charge everyone to think or do as I do. I acknowledge we are all in different places in our development in Christ. And you must hear God for yourself, your ministry, your assignments, and your "how to". However, I can say this confidently: if you're going to travel, especially internationally, you must believe in the provision of our Heavenly Father. I mean, why not ask God if you should fly commercial or should you obtain a jet and a pilot? I realize that there is much work before us. A jet wouldn't necessarily be a luxury. It enables us to move expeditiously and maximize our time. He knows the right answer to that for each ministry.

Imagine what could have been accomplished if the first-century apostles had jets? How much lighter would the burden have been in traveling to assignments? The apostles always depended upon the Lord to be their source. You never heard them begging for resources. They trusted the Lord to get things done. So, as Kingdom pollinators, they weren't handicapped by a lack of finances when it was time to go and strengthen the saints. Hallelujah. Don't let whether you have income start or stop you in your future. **Discern the will of God and go for it. The creation is waiting on you.**

> Pray as though everything depended on God.
> Work as though everything depended on you.
> — Augustine

CHAPTER FIVE

YOKEFELLOWS IN THE WORK

And I intreat thee also, true yokefellow, help
those women which laboured with me in the
gospel, with Clement also, and with other fellow
labourers, whose names are in the book of life.
Philippians 4:3

Let's get back into the word of God's Kingdom. I shared in the last chapter concerning *the work.* I also shared some personal experiences with you. I want to focus more on the scripture and experiences in this chapter. I stated earlier that walking in faith is the first aspect of doing the work. We know this from Hebrews 11:6, "But without faith, it is impossible to please Him: For he that cometh to God must believe that he is and that he is a rewarder of them that diligently seek him." The rule of faith never changes, regardless of how much we grow or experience. The Bible tells us to grow in faith. So, faith should never diminish. It should be growing daily.

Now let's go back for a moment and consider John 6. How many of you are pastoring or leading a ministry? Who among you are leaders in business? Who among you are leading a family? Can you relate to their thoughts and questions? Look at it again.

> Then said they unto him, "What shall we do,
> that we might work the works of God?" (v. 28)

That was a legitimate question. What should we do? How can *we* do these things? Generally, we think in terms of doing first rather than being. We should reverse that, understanding that doing comes out of believing. Our being is based in what God has said. Our doing should be based on believing that. "Jesus answered and said to them, 'This is the work of God, that you believe in Him whom He sent'" (v. 29).

Jesus put everything in context. His answer provides the first and most essential step in doing the work of God. The message in John 6 was first given to the Jews in the first century. What about us? What about you?

You're responsible for the work God has given you to launch. Whether your assignment is sacred or secular, people will come to you with their questions just as they came to Jesus. You must have enough faith to say, "You must believe in me whom the Lord has sent." I want you to think about that for a moment because you must be confident that **God** has sent you. You're not out here alone. I implore you to have confidence that God sent you. And then, as people receive you, it will be easy for you to tell them to believe in you as a sent one from the Heavenly Father. Always remember this isn't arrogance when spoken out of humility and truth knowing you are accountable to be led by His Spirit.

So, be aware that the enemy is out to sabotage your confidence. When we first came to Florida at the leading of the Lord, I had to remind myself that God sent us. We often encountered voices of doubt and unbelief, voices that were speaking contrary to the truth we knew. We were sent ones. I had to disregard those voices of doubt and remain in faith to what God had said. All that matters is, "What has God spoken?" When you are certain, you can stand firm and speak as boldly as Jesus. Believe on the one that God has sent.

Someone may say, "Jesus was original! And brother, you aren't Jesus!" When that happens, you ask yourself this: "Who are you?" You must know who's working in and with you. This is when *a clear identity is a must*. Without hesitation, we must learn to say He is the first among many sons—we are joint-heirs with Christ. We must leave the teachings that hinder us from knowing who we are.

In John 14:23, "Jesus answered and said unto him, 'If a man love me, he will keep my words: and my Father will love him, and we will come unto him, and make our abode with him.'" Jesus was speaking about the baptism of the Holy Spirit. One becomes the residence of the Godhead in that experience.

It wasn't that you received the Holy Spirit as a separate entity. Is that a new thought to you?

Look at that again: "My father and I, we will come and make our abode." In other words, we become the house of God. The Word of God tells us that the fullness of the Godhead bodily was in Jesus. And the same fullness came when the Father, the Son, and the Holy Spirit came to live in you. This should be our normal way of thinking. We should thank Paul for revealing this to us in Philippians 2:5–6: "Let this mind be in you, which was also in Christ Jesus: Who, being in the form of God, thought it not robbery to be equal with God." Paul told them to "see to it" that this mindset was resident in them. This is not a strange modern or post-modern Christian mindset.

No, go back to the Word of God. Look at what the Word says. And when it comes to you obeying God and stepping forward into the work, don't be afraid to say to people, "You should believe in me, the one whom the Father has sent." I want that to sink in for the moment. When you're talking about the work of the Lord, Jesus said,

> For I say unto you, "Ye shall not see me henceforth, till ye shall say, 'Blessed is he that cometh in the name of the Lord.'" (Matthew 23:39)

The name speaks of the nature or character of the Lord. When it comes to your assignment, you must execute it only in the name of the Lord. Paul said, "And whatsoever you do in word or deed, do all in the name of the Lord Jesus, giving thanks to God and the Father by Him" (Colossians 3:17). Many desire to see Jesus. *Let them see Him in you.* And, if they reject you (the sent one), they reject the one who sent you. The Lord Jesus Christ has ascended and remains in His seated position. His seat is in the invisible realm of the Spirit. Many want Him to leave that position and come to receive them because they want to see Jesus. They are failing to see Him in His Body. Some are actually openly refusing to see Him in His Body for want of a spectacular appearing of the supernatural. To that we ask, "Would you recognize Him as He comes? How do you know what He looks like?" We can't depend on the renditions of artists. Any artist's rendering is mere human speculation about Jesus' appearance before the crucifixion.

What does the Word say? This is what we do know: Jesus lives in His people, right here and right now. *He chooses to present Himself through the corporate body of Christ.* This is how you will see Him for now. He doesn't come just once or twice. He is the ever-present One. He comes many times in many expressions.

Let's take that even further. You and I, as we mature, we are among the many ways He presents Himself! I know this is a powerful consideration, but you must believe it! He died as a seed corn to multiply Himself into an unlimited full ear of corn. As we truly believe this, the revelation brings deep humility and responsibility. These are the hallmarks of maturing sons, the evidence of maturing ones who are not ashamed of the gospel of Christ living in them, as Him.

So, in Acts 13, we see that the assignment is worth searching and seeking out. The assignees are properly developed and released to do the assignment. That was one thing Apostle Sanders, my pastor, would do with the young preachers that I grew up with. We all wanted to preach, and that's not an evil thing. When one is truly called of God for the Word ministry, the desire to teach and preach will be there. However, we needed nurturing to develop our gifts and mature our souls.

There was a certain period of development before he released us. He would let us know if we needed further work. In our meetings, he would say, "Boys, you're not quite ready yet." We lost several ministers over that statement. Now some of us were graced and wise enough to hang around. It didn't mean we liked that decision; it meant that we had enough confidence in him that he was telling us the truth. We needed what he was saying at that moment!

Running prematurely into ministry can produce some disastrous consequences. However, at some point, every called person must be released to run with their calling! By experience, we found Apostle Sanders' instructions to be true. They came alive in me when I became a pastor. There is a time for your release into a greater level of fullness.

Most people don't appreciate the things parents say when they're younger and teenagers. Many times, we're left wondering why they say certain things. Then, you get married and start to produce a family. The children grow up and become teenagers. You listen to what they say, and it vaguely reminds you of someone else— yourself! Does it shock you that you are becoming your mom and dad in your responses to your children? It really shouldn't shock any of us.

After becoming a parent and pastor, I knew what he was talking about because critical areas of development are essential to the work. We can see some of this happening before Acts 13, as Barnabas and Saul prepared for the work for many years. They had walked through the discovery and development phases of ministry. Now, they have come to the deployment phase. They were deployed as a team with a common yoke.

Deployment with a common yoke can be best illustrated by observing military forces. Nations spend millions in equipment and thousands of hours of development to yoke their troops together. Because they know at some point they are going to be deployed and their lives (and many others) may depend upon the security of that yoke.

Let's go back to the word yoked. Barnabas and Saul became yokefellows. That meant they were in union with each other. They were not pulling apart from each other but pulling together. A colleague is a modern term for this operation. Such a person is considered to have equal value to the operation with the one who considers them a colleague.

Allow me to describe a yoke that was placed on plowing animals. The band of a yoke is a U-shape placed on the neck of each animal. There was a wooden bar that connected the two. Figuratively, the wood that connected Barnabas and Saul was the Holy Ghost. He was the only one that could keep them connected. What's going to keep any of us connected? It's the same Holy Ghost that kept them!

The word *yokefellow* comes from the Greek term *suzugos*[7]. In English, we spell it *syzygy*. You may be asking, "What is a syzygy?" Webster defines it as "the nearly straight-line configuration of three celestial bodies (such as the sun, moon, and earth during a solar or lunar eclipse) in a gravitational system[8]. So, when you're yoked as co-laborers, you acknowledge that you are lined together. No one is lagging or attempting to get ahead. You're laboring together. The scripture tells us don't be like the horse or the mule (Psalm 32:9; paraphrased). The horse is fast and maybe impetuous, and the mule is slow and possibly stubborn. You can't be in a horse-mule relationship when you're starting a ministry together. That's not good! We must remain co-yoked in our assignment. If you go back to the original two people co-yoked in the dominion assignment, it was the male and the female in the image of God. So, what did this sinister serpent do? He put room between what God had joined together. In the mind of God, *nothing is to come between what He had joined.*

Why do you think the struggle is so intense and so real between males and females? It goes back to the Garden of Eden. Why come up with sayings like, "men are from Mars, and women are from Venus?" What is behind this saying? That comes from the observation that there is often counterproductive, yoke-breaking room allowed or intentionally placed between the two.

But the good news is that Calvary closed the gap and placed us back together! Now, we can labor together rather than against one another. Laboring together makes you (us) yokefellows. Paul, in Philippians 4:3, said this: "And I intreat thee also, true yokefellow, help those women which laboured with me in the gospel, with Clement also, and with other my fellowlabourers, whose names are in the book of life." There's much in this verse, but clearly, something was going on, and help was needed. Satan was attempting to put asunder **what God had joined together.**

Notice that Paul didn't hound them. He didn't set them down. He said, "Help them!" Paul recognized their benefit in the gospel, not only to him but also to Clement and many other fellow laborers recorded in the book of life. So, he was speaking to this true yokefellow. The scripture doesn't give us his identity. However, we know that he's one of many yokefellows that Paul shared.

As the apostles moved in their assignment, I want you to see something very important. Acts 13:5 (NAS) says, "When they reached Salamis, they began to proclaim the word of God in the synagogues of the Jews; and they also had John as their helper." Here's the statement. The previous people of God (the Jews) were granted the first opportunity to receive the gospel. Generally, they rejected the preaching of the gospel. Afterward, Paul's practice was to go to the Gentiles. Those first selected of God in another season needed upgrading. All of us must remember there's something beyond what we know.

Every person and every group only know *in part*. It is arrogant and juvenile to think that we only need to hear over and over the part we have. God has so designed the Body that we must be open to learn from others. And, we must be willing to learn without calling things heresy simply because they are different than what we already know. That only opens us up to offense and the temptation to persecute someone or something that could be of vital importance to our growth! Again, all of us must remember there's something beyond what we know.

From this same passage, the next thing to look at is that John Mark was chosen to minister to the apostles. I don't see any place in scripture where the Holy Ghost said, "Separate John Mark with Barnabas and Paul." I want you to think about this because this will become a contention a little bit later. Some things in life were at their discretion as mature men of God. Adding Mark to their team was one of those discretionary moments. And they initially agreed that he would accompany them.

The Greek word used for *minister* in this Acts 13 passage is ***huperetes***. Actually, seven different words are used in the New Testament for our single word servant (or minister), and this is one of them. *Huperetes* means an under-rower or an under-oarsman[9]. Enslaved people, and frequently, soldiers captured as prisoners of war, served as under-rowers. They would man the oars of the Triremes, which were ships with three decks. The rowers propelled the boats. A person's station determined which of the three levels they rowed from. The group on the lowest level was called the under-rowers. This level was manned by those captured in warfare. That was going to be their lot for the rest of their lives. They were usually chained to their post and hardly ever saw daylight. They constantly heard the barking of a commander telling them what speed to row.

John Mark was their under-rower. This did not work out well at all. Acts 13:13 says, "Now when Paul and his company loosed from Paphos, they came to Perga in Pamphylia: and John (Mark) departing from them returned to Jerusalem." Does that sound to you like somebody chained to that post for the rest of their lives? No! But notice, it *didn't* say that the apostles Barnabas and Paul sent him away. *He chose* to leave on his own.

Perhaps he didn't care for being the under-rower. Perhaps he didn't receive enough recognition or status? Perhaps he felt undervalued or that his gifts were not appreciated or respected—sound familiar? Or perhaps the journey was too difficult. We can only imagine these things because of human tendencies. But wisdom teaches us that presumption nearly always leads to offense.

What we can safely do is solidly remain with what scripture tells us, in the case of John Mark and in our own lives. So, what did they do? They let him go. And when anybody tells you, "The Lord told me my season here is up," or, "I think God is leading me to leave you." You have one choice as a leader: Let them go! If you've never experienced those words as a leader, you will. Don't get upset and make presumptions when you hear them—give God room to work.

Now here's part of the struggle. John Mark is Barnabas' nephew. After reading and observing Paul's temperament, you know he will not easily forget this moment. Barnabas had already forgiven him when the time came to take the next apostolic mission. He was able to let it go. He was ready to take this young servant on the next missionary trip. Paul said, "I don't think so!" What did he remember? John Mark bailed out on them the first time. The scripture doesn't indicate what prompted that decision. Maybe it was a moment of deep suffering, and Mark wasn't prepared for that. And he says, "I'm out of here!" Paul remembered this. When it's time to go again, he's in no mood to take Mark with them.

There will be all kinds of reasons people leave you. I don't know what Mark's situation was here, but here's the deal. When a person is young and immature, he or she will make immature decisions. Don't hold it over their heads for a lifetime. Let it go. Leave them a soft place to land. As we said before, years later, Paul had a different opinion of John Mark. He declared him as profitable. What happened in Mark's life? He had grown. And so had Paul.

Now, if your personality is that way, this is the word of the Lord to you today. "Get over it! Forgive it. Move past that." You're working with people who are developing and maturing. Many times, they don't catch it the first go-round. So just hang in there with them until they do.

Fear God and work hard.
— David Livingstone

CHAPTER SIX
MINISTRY PROTOCOL

Trust in the LORD with all thine heart; and lean
not unto thine own understanding. In all thy ways
acknowledge him, and he shall direct thy paths
Proverbs 3:5–6

B arnabas and Saul were released and set forth by the Holy
Ghost to do **the work** they had been called to do. They
didn't give the work a particular name at first. They just called
it *the work*. After the prophets and teachers fasted and prayed,
they laid hands on them and released them to God's work.
Holy Spirit was directing their paths.

Apostolic order is revealed in the verses from Acts 13 and
Proverbs 3, along with others. If you're going to be orderly, this
is the right process. Any of us can choose to send ourselves.

But the order of God is that the sender should be someone of greater or equal authority in the Spirit. They should be there to assist in the laying on of hands. Participation by other elders signifies agreement. This is called a presbytery. We're saying we agree with God's choice at this special time.

There should be someone that knows you in a presbytery service. That is God's way. Now, I can tell you it was that way for me. Although I was somewhat aware of what God wanted from me, I refused to go forth in ministry until the agreement was in Apostle Sanders. There was also agreement in the other men of God that I labored with for many years. Apostle Sanders summoned the other apostles in the region. Together, they laid hands on us and released us to the work of the Kingdom.

I am confident and firmly persuaded that I'm not somewhere bitter and upset because of our course of action. There's enough in the work that could get you bitter and upset. When I arrived in Southwest Florida, the greeting committee wasn't encouraging. They said, "Well if you last two years, we'll know that you have something from God." What a greeting! I didn't hear one word about we're glad you're here to help bring in the harvest.

After two years passed, they wanted to inspect for two more years. Now it's been more than thirty-six years. I haven't heard from my greeters anymore. Most of them are no longer in the area. I have been sustained by the grace of God and the foundations of my sending. When a person steps through the front door into ministry, that's the proper way. No one should step through the side door or back door because of anger or irritation with God's set person in their lives. Suppose you are moving out of or into a place of ministry because of anger, offense, or irritation. In that case, you are mixing up a recipe for disaster.

I love something a fellow minister said, "*The same pants that you got mad in, you can also get glad in.*" No person benefits from living life while holding onto offense and anger. In Matthew chapter 5, Jesus taught powerfully about anger. He dealt with anger with and without a cause, knowing that anger fuels the spirit of murder. Murder may happen physically or with the mouth. Paul said it this way in Ephesians 4:26: "*Be ye angry, and sin not: let not the sun go down upon your wrath: Neither give place to the devil.*" Anger isn't something anyone should go to sleep with. The consequences are too devastating for the human body.

Anyone who yields to anger has a maximum of twelve hours to be upset; you must get rid of it. You must forgive. I know you're laughing, but I'm serious about this. You got about 12 hours to deal with it, and that is if it happens first thing at sunrise! You don't want to go to sleep in anger. Not once. Did you know that in doing so, you allow destruction to be absorbed into your spirit, your soul (mind, will, and emotions), and your physical cells? What happens if you do? My wife Michelle has studied this and knows this subject well. Her studies confirmed that if we give place to the devil and violate the scriptures, it could take days and months to bring the body back into healthy equilibrium. I completely agree with the scripture and her. Don't let the sun go down on your wrath!

Anger should never be why we go into or out of the work of the Kingdom. It's the wrong reason, and it's never the right one. When the Holy Ghost releases someone, that's the right reason. You have opened a pipeline for the Holy Spirit's leading even when you don't know everything in your assignment. Maturity is denoted in a son of God when they live life in this manner.

We may have ministry plans. However, the Holy Spirit has the right to interrupt them. He will release an aspect of His plan that we weren't considering. Many messages have been preached on Paul's Macedonian call recorded in Acts 16. That was an occasion of a divine interruption. Paul and Silas had planned to visit the churches planted on a previous missionary trip. Their purpose was to establish further and confirm the saints.

Before they arrived at the churches, Paul received the Macedonian call. The gravity of this call had not fully registered. God was simply looking for Paul's yes to a divine interruption to their plans. This was the first opportunity for the gospel to enter Europe. No, this wasn't the first time the Gentiles were ministered to. That happened in Acts 10. The gospel of the Kingdom was released into an entirely different field. Thus far, Kingdom work has been done in Asia. Through Paul and Silas' obedience, it is now in Europe. Afterward, the continent of Europe became a haven for the gospel of the Kingdom.

Right now, we are benefiting from that one act of obedience. The gospel traveled from Europe with the persecuted separatists to America in the seventeenth century. So, there is much about the work that we may not see at first. However, all who go must know that they were authorized and sent. The Heavenly Father sent Jesus; Jesus sent the eleven apostles, and the Holy Ghost sent Barnabas and Saul. *Each of these was a ministry call into the apostleship.*

I'm amazed that every time I see the word *apostle* in the New Testament, it is never spelled with a capital letter. Have you ever paid attention to that? It is always spelled with a small "*a*." Why is that? God doesn't want us to get hung up on titles. **Emphasis on function is more important than emphasizing titles**. When the first apostles drifted in that direction, Jesus reminded them they were all brothers. That immediately de-emphasized pecking orders and position-seeking.

A few times in the past, I had ministers stop me in my tracks and correct me because I didn't address them as Apostle or Prophet. I accommodated them because that was a need in their lives. Although that wasn't an issue, I complied because I didn't want my meat to offend my brethren. It is easier to drop down a few notches until our brothers rise.

Now note that I am not speaking of denying honor where honor is due. Deference and reference are ways of honor. And we should teach those coming up to excel in respect and to honor elders and authority. The Word says that God honors those who honor Him (1 Samuel 2:30). When we honor parents, elders, and those in authority above us, we are honoring the Word. It actually states that those who bring the Word to us (five-fold ministers) are worthy of double honor (1 Timothy 5:17). So those should be taught to our children and our spiritual children as nonnegotiable givens. Instead, where I am speaking above of "emphasis on function is more important than emphasizing titles," I am addressing the inappropriate need to demand honor or title for *yourself*.

We're also communicating these foundations in our leaders' summits and ministry schools because some have decided that there were no more apostles or prophets after the first century. Rather, traveling ministries were called missionaries. Female ministers were also only called missionaries in the branch of Pentecost I associated with in my younger development. They usually wore white and were recognized for having spiritual authority. But there was something we didn't know about the word *missionary*. It came from the Latin word *missio*, which was like *apostello*. If you go back to classical Hebrew, it was the word *shalach*. A person sent by someone greater was called a *shaliah*. The shaliah was someone sent on an errand. In Genesis 24, Eliezer became Abraham's shaliah. He was sent to receive a wife for Isaac, Abraham's son. How many of you would have appreciated your dad choosing your wife or husband? Cultural-ly, we can't relate to that. It was very common and still is in the east. But the charge—it was a profound responsibility.

Abraham charged Eliezer, and Eliezer received the charge. The scripture tells us that he was Abraham's eldest servant. He didn't send someone immature. (I hope your name is not Johnny. If so, forgive me for using this name, but this is just an illustration.) Abraham didn't send immature Johnny because he could run fast. He sent someone who was going to carry out the assignment. **The only thing that mattered was for the**

shaliah to carry out the assignment. And *to do so in the way it was instructed to be completed.* The assignment was paramount to all else.

Upon arrival, Eliezer would not even eat until he made known his mission. Eliezer refused a common courtesy because of the importance of His mission. He said, "*I will not eat until I have told mine errand*" (Genesis 24:33). The Hebrew word for the errand is *dabar*. The servant made it known that he must release the word he was sent to release. I (we) must do no less!

When speaking of the assignment, *we're supposed to release the Word.* That must be just as important to me when I travel on assignments as it was to Eliezer. Of course, I enjoy eating. One glance at me (or our social media posts) will tell you that! I don't look like I'm withering away. I do enjoy good meals. But when it's an assignment, I have the same mindset that Jesus had: "*I have meat to eat that ye know not of*" (John 4:32). Full concentration is given to the delivery of God's Word. So, in this manner, we see that Eliezer was a powerful representative of the three words: shaliah, apostle, and missionary. His full commitment was to the word he carried and the mission he was sent to do in the way he was instructed.

Let's consider the order of the apostles. First, there is Jesus, the chief apostle. I get tickled when I go into a region with a thousand apostles. Somebody is going to take on the title of chief apostle. Brethren, we're not supposed to be liars. The only one that qualifies to be the chief apostle is Jesus. Everybody else carries *some* of Him. That's why he made *some* apostles and some prophets. As long as we continue in Him, we are delivering our portion of Him, the chief apostle, and there will always be others who carry and contribute their portion of the oil and the spice.

All servants receive a portion of the full expression of Jesus. We might as well decapitate Goliath and his brothers while dealing with this. When you hear somebody say "the greatest prophet," know that there's only one: Jesus. Everyone else gets some of His prophetic anointing and grace. The chief apostle, Jesus, is still speaking to those with ears to hear and hearts that are open and receptive to His voice.

So, mature and realize that you're only carrying *some* of Him as you move forward. In recognizing that, you'll be eager and willing to work with others who carry *some* of Him. Say it with me: "*Some for each of us and all only in all of us!*" We share Him. This ensures that the full expression of Christ in the earth comes from *the corporate expression*—the fellowship of His Body expressing Him as One.

I'll give you another example of how ego and self-conceit can get in the way. There have been situations of convening apostles in the past. The lead apostle declared that there would be one chair in the room, and everybody else would sit on the floor. Beware when you hear or witness things like this, but don't be alarmed if you run into people like this. How do you handle it? The same way that God handled the uprising of Lucifer. He responded oppositely. Through Jesus Christ, God stooped very low, whereas Lucifer attempted to arise. That's how you handle this kind of stuff. Jesus was powerful and confident in His assignment and position. Yet, He was meek and lowly. This brings us back to where I was in previous chapters...

> The true attitude in which you learn Kingdom
> things is meekness.

Meekness doesn't mean weakness. It simply means that you're even-keeled and not up-and-down like a yo-yo in your soul. I'm not talking about pretense. I'm talking about the real deal—men and women in whom the Holy Ghost has worked with evidence of Him working in their lives. When you meet them, you should immediately recognize godly humility. You're looking at someone who has taken on a learning yoke because that's how you learn the way of *God's Kingdom*.

When sent by the Holy Ghost, He becomes our source. We must be more dependent on Him than anyone or anything else. This is foundational before we frame the rest of the building. We cannot put the rest of the building together without this foundation.

When we first came to Southwest Florida, I was financially weak, although I had an abundance of the Word of God. I had one choice and one choice only. I had to depend on the Holy Ghost to be my source. Today, I can share the truth that I learned back then. When you start your assignments, there might be times you are tempted to seek other sources. This is what you must remember. There is only one that qualifies as your source, and that's God through the Holy Ghost. He may use others as channels. God may use many outlets or channels to get you what he wants you to have. But always remember *He's your source.*

On my way to Cape Coral, Florida, my thinking had to adjust quickly. I had never paid more than $200 per month for rent. That's unheard of today but wasn't unheard of in January 1986. We arrived in the heart of the tourist season when everything was more expensive. Complaining (in my mind) to the Lord, I thought He could have sent me in the summer. Things would be cheaper in the summer because the tourists are gone. However, it didn't happen that way. Was this a time when my faith had to increase in God's ability? Yes! Since faith comes by hearing God's Word, I needed to hear the voice of God.

I traveled on Piedmont Airlines to get to Cape Coral. (Do any of you remember that now-defunct airline?) We were at cruising altitude, and I began to pray quietly. *"Father, what do I look for once I arrive in Cape Coral?"* He placed a figure in my head, twice the amount I had paid in North Carolina. That's why I needed an expansion in faith. The work of the Lord for me was to believe in God's ability. Before I preached a sermon or taught a lesson, I had to have faith in God's provision. I had to hold to the truth that faith comes by hearing and hearing by the word of God.

I swallowed hard when I heard those numbers because it wasn't like God would change his mind. Also, it wasn't like the circumstances in Southwest Florida were going to change within a few hours before I arrived. After arriving, I asked my host, "Can I find a place to live at this price?" He took me to the ghetto. I had a wife and children joining me in Florida soon! I politely asked him to get me out of there as quickly as possible. We looked in other places. Shortly we found another place. When you follow the leading of the Holy Spirit, He will help you. He led us to a beautiful neighborhood. I felt the Holy Spirit's witness that a certain house in that neighborhood was the right one. Did I know that was the place other than being led by the Spirit of God? No! When doing Kingdom work, you must be led by the Holy Spirit.

I asked my host to take me to a realtor to speak with someone. The realtor showed me the house and asked if I liked it. I answered, "Oh yes!" She informed me of the normal rent price for that home during the season. It was four times what I generally paid for rent. I remembered the exact price God gave me on the plane at that time. It was half the amount the realtor had quoted me. I had to forget what was in my head and allow faith to rise. The realtor followed up by saying, "But we will rent you the home for $xxx.xx" —*the exact price God had spoken to me on the plane.* Hallelujah!

I was young and willing to trust God implicitly. One of the dangers of getting older is thinking too much; you start thinking about all you have walked through. Never lose sight that God is your source. That day, I learned a very important lesson while looking for our first housing in Cape Coral. None of the math figures matter when God sends you to do Kingdom work! From that day onward, I established that God is our source, and He leads us in all wisdom. He will use other people to bring His supply, but they are merely channels—He alone remains our source. God is our Source and Supply; if and only as we remain connected to Him, to the Source and Supply, we become resources and resupply carriers for God's Kingdom!

Over the years, different supporters of the ministry have come and gone. God never allowed us to get locked into one channel. The Father eventually brought in some substantial channels. But one must never forget that The Heavenly Father resources kingdom work. There is no lack in him, period. Even if he must send you fishing, the provision will be in the fish's mouth. Again, what are we learning? We are joined to Him, and we will do nothing without Him. Second, he is our source and our provision. God will not allow us to flirt with idolatry by trusting other channels. *We will walk that reality daily as our steps are ignited for future assignments.* Regardless of where He leads us, we must trust Him.

One of my go-to scriptural verses is Proverbs 3:5: "Trust in the LORD with all thine heart; lean not unto thine own understanding." The Lord is telling us two great truths. Trust Him with our hearts and resist the urge to lean into our understanding, knowing how limited it is. The older we get, the more we realize our natural limitations. So, when you're talking about being launched into Kingdom work like Barnabas and Saul, you cannot afford to lean into any area of your own understanding. They had to trust that God would direct their path.

Trust is the glue of life. It's the most essential ingredient in effective communication. It's the foundational principle that holds all relationships.
— Stephen R. Covey

CHAPTER SEVEN

WHAT GOD HAS JOINED TOGETHER

What therefore God hath joined together,
let not man put asunder.
Mark 10:9

To be yoked is to be joined together. Let's look at this from Matthew 19:3–8. The text begins with the Pharisees testing Jesus:

> The Pharisees also came unto him, tempting him and saying unto him, "Is it lawful for a man to put away his wife for every cause?" And he answered and said unto them, "Have ye not read, that he which made them at the beginning made them male and female, and said, for

this cause shall a man leave father and mother, and shall cleave to his wife: and they twain shall be one flesh? Wherefore they are no more twain, but one flesh. What therefore God hath joined together, let not man put asunder." They say unto him, "Why did Moses then command to give a writing of divorcement and to put her away?" He saith unto them, "Moses, because of the hardness of your hearts, suffered you to put away your wives: but from the beginning, it was not so."

These men asked Jesus if it is legal to dismiss one's wife for any cause, justifiable or not. That indicated the hardness of their hearts. Jesus answered by taking them back to the original mandate in the book of Genesis. That mandate had no corrupt files or twisted views—it was straight from God's heart. His answer wasn't based on prevailing philosophies or cultural nuances. God had a perfect plan for males and females in the beginning. This settles the case because Jesus, the Word made flesh, talks to us from a perspective as the eternal Word of God.

This answer is not modernism, post-modernism, or futurism. How did God make the first people? Did He make a male and a female? Yes! Father God made two distinct humans. They were made with no genetic anomalies. Those only began after Adam disobeyed his Heavenly Father. Jesus made it clear that a man abandons his father and mother for a woman, not another man. She becomes his wife in the process. He shall cleave to his wife, and they become one flesh. *Cleave* means *to glue together.* The intent was to create an inseparable joining. They are glued so tightly that they become a duo, the concept of two becoming one. They are no more separate but one flesh. Therefore, what God has joined together becomes one.

Joined together is the verb form of the noun *yoke.* **God joins people in a marriage to create a binding yoke between them.** When joined together in Christ, it is not just a union of man and wife, as in worldly marriages. Those yokes do not have real staying power. A man and woman will live together in a true tripartite yoke when joined in *holy* matrimony, with Christ being the bond, their union (spirit, soul, and body) becomes *the Savior's perfect yoke.*

I want you to underscore what Jesus *didn't* say. He did not say "who" God had joined together; it was "what" God has joined together. We all know that God didn't join some people who joined themselves together. **The purpose behind the joining is greater than the people. God joins people <u>for the greater good of the Kingdom</u>.** That is the reason marriage must be protected. We must allow nothing to place room between the bond or separate *what God has joined.*

I want to expand our view of this passage of scripture. There have been many examples of what God had joined together that people chose to put room between. But God was the one that had joined them.

Let's note the second question the Pharisees quizzed Jesus with (v. 7): "Why did Moses then command to give a writing of divorcement and to put her away?" Also, note that they did not speak of the man being put away. The talk was about putting *her* away, right? Jesus made it clear that Moses gave those commands because of the hardness of their hearts, *sklerokardia*[10], which means hardheartedness and destitution of spiritual perception. But from the beginning, it was not to be this way.

So now, let's look closely here. How do we respond when speaking about an issue with cultural and moral consequences? Notice what Jesus did. He went back to the beginning. This is important because there are many things that we're dealing with which have moral consequences today. **You cannot uproot God's original plan because of what has evolved through the generations.** Therefore, you must return to the beginning. There are no corrupt human files in the beginning.

The only thing you have in the beginning is The Word of God, which was (and is) the truth. So, that's why Jesus took this issue back to the beginning. It was that important. Always consider the beginning when searching for the unadulterated truth. The beginning is the first estate of any human matter. Jesus tells them (us) that they (we) have corrupt files in them (us) because of the hardness of heart. That's why Moses permitted certain behavior, but it was not so from the beginning.

Let's deal with two critical issues here. Because, again, we're in leaders' school. I know the Holy Spirit will lead you in implementation. God has a plan that shouldn't be tampered with or usurped. Whether it's a divergent plan or disobedience, it is still the work of the enemy. But here's the point. **What did God say when he first talked about man?** What did he say? We have a record of that in these verses:

Let us make man in our image, after our likeness: and let them have dominion over the fish of the sea, and over the fowl of the air, and over the cattle, and over all the earth, and over every creeping thing that creepeth upon the earth. (Genesis 1:26)

This is one of the most phenomenal statements ever spoken. It sets the tone for human DNA, and that DNA is spiritual as much as it is biological. We have a spiritual DNA coded with finishing, not with failure. You know what else? Your spiritual DNA has nothing to do with *independence* because God gave us the DNA of his *family.* We are speaking of things much larger than any individual. It's not all about me. For example, we must get beyond the mentality of seeking what this church can do *for us.* This is the typical conversation, internally if not externally: How will they bless me? How are they going to benefit me and my children? Me, me, me! *That was never the language in the beginning.*

So even from the context of looking at God, he's talking in terms of family. Man is the expressed image of God's *corporate reality.* Everything about man forms a yoke, a threefold cord. Every devilish activity behind the corrupt file is to steal, kill, and destroy the original design of the yoke. The strength of Adam's physical yoke was *obedience not independence.* So, you go back to the beginning and deal with this. That's why I share with the young pastors how to do this. I want them to deposit in people as much truth as possible about the beginning before anything got corrupt. That's what you want to establish in people solidly. Again, *the beginning was about a corporate man in the image of God.* Everyone contributing to the whole and well-being of the whole ensures that each individual is wholly cared for as well. You don't hear any singular pronouns in this command. They're all plural. He was already thinking about a vast family of fully developed sons. Paul would later say **we are to come into union with the current form of Christ** (Romans 8:29). Christ is the image of God and was there from the beginning. If you're an adversary, what are you going to do? Attempt to disconnect and divide.

The adversary's intent was to attempt to block them from carrying out the dominion mandate—get them disconnected from the source that gave them the mandate. How do you get disconnected from the source that gave you the mandate? Get them into a posture of doubt, disobedience, and disconnection. **It is impossible to fulfill the mandate if one is in a posture of doubt, disobedience, and disconnection.**

If you're going to **be fruitful, multiply, and replenish** the earth, you must stay in obedience. It will require God's grace for this mandate to be fulfilled. Thank you, Lord! I see abundance in those three words: fruitful, multiply, and replenish. I see nothing about poverty in those three words. Think about it. The enemy of your and my soul constantly tries to get us to think in terms of poverty. Here's how that might sound: How are we going to survive? What am I going to do? Why do others have more than me when I am faithful? Don't listen to the voice of fear, doubt, and unbelief!

We are going to survive and thrive. The Word of God says we will increase more and more (Psalm 115:14). I'm doing more than talking to myself and allowing you to listen. Thriving is one of the most basic promises for sons of God who will seek first the Kingdom. All things are added to obedient seekers. Father God created all things for our enjoyment. There is nothing to be anxious or fretful about. Leave apprehension behind. The Heavenly Father is our shield and exceeding great reward. He's our protection and provision. **God is for us, and it doesn't matter who's against us.** Hallelujah! Hallelujah! Why do we ever doubt Him? Why would we doubt him when He has placed his perfect yoke of love on our necks?

Jesus said, "*My yoke is easy, and my burden is light.*" Here's another way of saying the same thing: "I don't want you up all night fretting about how you're going to make it or how you are going to pay the bills." There are times in the past I gave these things substantial consideration. And then, there comes an unexpected check in the mail. I would look up to Heaven and say, "Why did I ever doubt You?"

I acknowledge that the Lord gave me Michelle to remind me of His faithfulness. Truthfully, I should never doubt Him. God wants us to step into each day, each new year, with this kind of confidence—freshly ignited with the confidence that He's always with us. He's always right there. As we comply with him, none of the adversary's suggestions matter. I'll tell you now that the vision inside you is far more enormous than what you have imagined. For that reason, in the next several chapters, I will say, "Wake up! Wake up and arise!"

Father God spoke this to Abraham after Lot was separated from him. The definition of Lot's name is ***veil***[11]. According to Hebrews 10:20, the veil is the flesh. Lot, the flesh man, was gone. The Lord said to him, "Lift now thine eyes" (Genesis 13:13). This is what the Spirit of God is also saying to us right now, "Wake up and look around. Look in every direction." Abraham was already standing in his inheritance and *had been there for a while*. He didn't know it until the removal of the flesh (Lot) and stripping of the veil to see clearly.

Think about the things you have seen. You aren't confined to seeing only from the church dimension. From the Tabernacle of Moses' perspective, a veil existed between the Holy Place and the Holiest-of-all. Think about what's available to be seen when the veil is removed. New things don't come from someplace; they're already there. In Christ, the veil is removed. It is gone. Get a hold of that. The veil. **What veil?** It is gone for those who are in Christ and will receive it. Don't rehang that curtain and blind your own view!

Certain realities are in you. It's just a matter of waking up and lifting your eyes roundabout—God has given you every benefit. Now, this is your assignment from Him. *Rise and start walking in everything I've given you.* And every place your feet touch is your possession.

What's the limitation? It is how much or how little ***you*** want to walk on. It isn't how much or how little you see. Remember, it was God who commanded him to look in every direction. So come on, you may see it all! *It will never benefit us if we choose not to walk in what we see.*

Well, glory to God. That stirs the preacher in me. Hallelujah! Being yoked together is the perfect template God placed in the earth as a visual. He wants the earth to reflect Heaven. The invisible God presented himself as three manifestations on the earth—the Father, the Son, and the Holy Spirit. They are *perfectly* yoked. He builds a man. He presents them as male and female. In Genesis 5:2, He calls their name Adam. Adam is a tripartite being—spirit, soul, and body. He was built to be yoked, *not* to be separated and independent. He built the male first, then brought the male and the female together. They were to be as yoked on earth **as** (meaning in the same manner that) the Father, the Son, and the Holy Spirit were in Heaven. Stop and let that sink in.

Ephesians 1:3–14 provides an extraordinary view of the Godhead in action. It is one sentence with breaks in between major thoughts. In the Greek language, you pause where we would place a period. Paul begins by talking about the administration of the Father and His embrace of His plan. The word, *embrace*, speaks of God *encircling* His plan. *It's a definitive word for a covenantal heart because God is a covenant keeper.* God provides meaningful touch to those He's in covenant with. *He embraces, surrounds, and enfolds us.* Paul speaks of how the Heavenly Father set this incredible plan in motion before the foundation of the world.

Then in Ephesians 1:7–12, he speaks about the Son of God. We see the administration of the Heavenly Father and His Son working together. They are yoked. The Son executes the Heavenly Father's plan. Execute means *to put into effect*. It is the validation of a legal document by performing the necessary formalities. Jesus came here to manifest and display all that was settled in the economy of the Godhead before there was anything. That's the legality of the Heavenly Father's covenant.

And then you have Ephesians 1:13–14, which talks about the administration of the Holy Spirit. We have been given the Holy Spirit of promise. We are sealed with Him until the fullness of the plan is completely worked out. We are presented with the Holy Spirit's stewardship in these verses. Stewardship speaks to an executive manager in the house. He is there to make sure (to guarantee) that we arrive to our expected end.

Now, we have the full picture. The Heavenly Father's **embrace**, the Son of God's **execution**, and the Holy Spirit's **aegis** (protection, safeguard, secure stewardship). This speaks of the power to plan, support, and protect until the plan is finished. Hallelujah!

That's what I call a perfect yoke—*The Savior's Perfect Yoke*. We have been allowed to walk perfectly yoked with God and one another. The Son of God declared the plan would work when He returned to the Heavenly Father and sat down enthroned. The eternal plan will work in the world and work in humanity.

Jesus could, without hesitation, say, "I'm the proof of it!" No devil, angel, or anyone else could disagree. Yes, and as *we* abide in, live, move, and have our being in Christ, *we also are the proof.* When we come to the culmination of the ages, angels won't be able to say, "Why did you choose a man?" That question will no longer linger. The Heavenly Father could have chosen angels. He could have made them compliant, yet He chose man. God gave him a will. He made humans like Himself. However, in the end, there will be no questions. The matter's conclusion will show that the new creation man brought his will into subjection to the Heavenly Father's will. Hallelujah!

The Holy Spirit of promise presently seals the deal! I want you to know that I can already hear things in my spirit. When something is sealed, it is like the natural canning process— whatever is inside is kept fresh, preserved. Paul wrote of Jesus' triumphant return to Glory. Paul said that Christ Jesus spoiled the principalities and powers, made a show of them openly, triumphing over them:

> Forasmuch then as the children are partakers of flesh and blood, he also himself likewise took part of the same; that through death he might destroy him that had the power of death, that is, the devil; And deliver them who through fear of death were all their lifetime subject to bondage. For verily he took not on him the nature of angels; but he took on him the seed of Abraham. (Hebrews 2:14-16)

Come on and say it with me, "The deal is sealed!" And in receiving Him, we are sealed by His Spirit. It is written, "Who hath also sealed us, and given the earnest of the Spirit in our hearts" (2 Corinthians 1:22). And in Ephesians 1:13, "In whom ye also trusted, after that ye heard the word of truth, the gospel of your salvation: in whom also after that ye believed, ye were sealed with that holy Spirit of promise…" And another, in Ephesians 4:30, "And grieve not the holy Spirit of God, whereby ye are sealed unto the day of redemption."

To finish this chapter, let's establish this: Father God has determined that the earth will have complete assurance of this matter. He's taking us back to the beginning of things. After many centuries of delay, He's showing us that He created them male and female in His image. They form a perfect yoke together with a Kingdom assignment in earth.

Humans were to be the first example of the *zygote*—the yoke. They were to work in tandem to understand the assignment and not take advantage of each other. There was to be no abnormal use of power by either one. They were created to be a dynamic duo (a power-filled duo). That was and is the plan of God.

God is One God, and males and females in the image of God are joined as one, In Him, to carry out His expression in this earth. When Adam, male and female, by their choice to disobey, failed in this assignment, they became unequally yoked with God *and* themselves. It demolished their obedience to the Father, putting room between their yoke with Him. We'll develop this further in the next chapter.

> Alone, we can do so little;
> together, we can do so much.
> — Helen Keller

CHAPTER EIGHT

YOKES OF BONDAGE

It is good for a man that he bear the yoke in his youth.
Lamentations 3:27

Let's get back into the word of God's Kingdom. In this study, we have dealt with the biblical concept of a yoke. Again, I want to emphasize this throughout our studies together: our steps are to display that His yoke is easy. Also, as we walk in humility, we learn that His burden is light. It's not heavy. We're moving forward in New Testament understanding. I want to deal with a few references *contrary* to the Lord's easy yoke.

The first one is in Acts 15:10. It is important to understand the backdrop of Acts 15. The gospel has advanced into the nations, the *ethnos¹²*. They are referred to as *Gentile nations*. This doesn't speak particularly of a single people group. Jerusalem,

93

Judea, and Samaria have been reached with the good news. Now, it is going into the utmost parts of the world. So, each of the four quadrants has heard the gospel. The number four is the number for universal view. So, the gospel of the Kingdom is a message with a universal reach. Jesus commanded us to go to all the world. It happened in the past, and it's happening now. The Lord planned it that way. Although highly successful locally, it was never the Lord's intent for them to stay in Jerusalem. They were to go, be fruitful, and multiply!

Here is the point. *God's plan has always been to establish His family and to multiply His presence in the earth.* How does that tie in to our chapter on yokes of bondage?

We don't build mature sons to keep them all at home. That would be a yoke of bondage. Can you hear this? Leaders? Can you hear the Spirit? Some will stay home, and others will go. The sooner you grasp this, the better leader you will be and the less vulnerable you will be to offense when the Lord sends others out from you.

It is not betrayal when sons and daughters grow up in the house of God and have a desire to be sent forth into ministry. This should be what we hope develops in their hearts! In fact, this is a good sign of a healthy ministry, raising generations!

As leaders (and as followers of Christ, the pattern Son) we can see plainly that the pattern of a spiritual family is similar to raising children in our personal home. The intent is to raise them so that they mature and develop into adults with compassion and integrity who desire to contribute to the world around them. The pattern all along was to go, be fruitful, and multiply.

They do this as they grow up, establish homes and careers of their own, and extend the family through their marriages and children. Grandchildren are the greatest blessing! Michelle and I have five and cherish each of them! We are thrilled that our children are growing the family. Why should it be different in the family of God, the house of God? We should recognize this as good and assist them! Grow the family!

There are 7.5 billion people in this world, and many have never heard the gospel of Jesus Christ. Many in developing countries don't even know there is a Gospel. And still, many who know of Jesus do not yet know there is a *Gospel of the Kingdom.*

In Acts 16, the men in Ephesus didn't know anything beyond John's baptism. They were unaware the previous season was completed. The Son of God had completed His mission, returned to Heaven, and sent the Holy Spirit. That's how far behind these men were. It is very important that the gospel stretch beyond the original group that received it. In this case, it had reached beyond the original group, but had not yet reached these men in Ephesus.

This is an example of how men (humanity) can hold on to elements of the former religious culture. John the baptizer came at the end of the Law Age. The age of the New Covenant proceeded (came after) the Law. Now, they were upgrading the information they had learned under the Law. Some very important teachings had to be worked out of them. I could just as easily say some had to be washed out through the washing of the water by the Word of God. In the transition from the old to the new, they were stubborn about certain teachings, such as physical circumcision and keeping other aspects of the Law of Moses. Does this sound familiar to things we encounter in the modern day church?

The first-century Jews had very little desire to come into Christ. The ones who did, many from pharisaic backgrounds, struggled mightily releasing all aspects of the Law. That created conflict and contention between the apostles, elders, and teachers. So how did they settle this? Thankfully, they came together rather than straying from each other.

The apostles and elders convened for their first council in Acts 15. The Holy Spirit released wisdom through the apostle James, preventing the church from fracturing. The leaders in the church would come together in later centuries to settle different things at different times. In one of them, Emperor Constantine brought some bishops together to maintain unity in the church. The Nicaean Code came out of one of those summits. The bishops settled different issues about the Trinity. They constructed a statement the church continues to use today.

Listen, many of them had suffered greatly; some were offended by colleagues; others had been physically abused by those that opposed the gospel's message. Perhaps some thought their way of thinking was the only right way. Does this sound familiar?

Peter had been used by God in the midst of that first council (in Acts 15). This happened because the Holy Spirit had done something totally unexpected in Peter's life. Heaven downloaded a vision that would change the world. It was a vision of all the people (including the *unclean*) that the apostolic message would touch. This was an inclusive vision. I'm only speaking of the inclusivity of all nations to receive Christ. Let's refresh ourselves with what happened in Acts 10 when Peter first received that vision:

> Peter went up upon the housetop to pray about the sixth hour: And he became very hungry, and would have eaten: but while they made ready, he fell into a trance and saw heaven opened, and a certain vessel descending unto him, as it had been a great sheet knit at the four corners, and let down to the earth: wherein were all manner of four-footed beasts of the earth, and wild beasts, and creeping things, and fowls of the air. And there came a voice to him, "Rise, Peter; kill, and eat." But Peter said, "Not so, Lord, for I have never eaten anything that is common or unclean." And the voice spake unto him again the second time, "What God hath cleansed, that call not thou common." This was done thrice: and the vessel was received up again into heaven. (Acts 10:9–16)

Allow me to give you a modern rendering of that event. How many of you know anything about **wrinkled steak**, often called **chitterlings** (pork intestines)? They are called **chitlins** by rural people. Imagine God lowering a knitted sheet from the heavens loaded with chitlins. He tells you to "Rise, slay, and eat!" Do you think you would feel like Peter? He responded, "Not so, Lord, because nothing like this has ever touched my lips, much less eaten it." I'm trying to give you a visual of what took place that day. Three times the command came to Peter. God told him, "What I've cleansed, don't you call common."

Peter pondered the matter. He was searching for understanding. He knew the dietary requirements established in the Law of Moses. Peter was certain you didn't eat anything on that sheet. The season has changed. Not only has the season changed, but there is also now a new normal. He's pondering that and trying to figure out what this is all about.

Next, Cornelius' representatives came seeking Simon, whose surname is Peter. If Peter had not been under the authority of the Holy Spirit, he would have been concerned. He was staying with Simon, the Tanner, at the time. He probably would have said, "Oh God, don't let this get back to the brothers in Jerusalem. I'm not even supposed to stay with a tanner; he's unclean." Can you see this as a setup from God?

Peter went to Cornelius' house and preached the gospel. He recognized for the first that God is no respecter of persons. In other words, God does not regard any man's face. If you are compliant with His will, you will receive all that God wants you to receive. Hallelujah.

Peter recognized that, as he preached, the Lord baptized Cornelius' household in the Holy Spirit. They could not forbid them from being water baptized. He faced a dilemma: he must take this message back to the brothers in Jerusalem. He could assure them that he wasn't seeking what happened with the Gentiles. He wasn't in full control of how everything went down. He had encountered God's preeminence, which is His primacy and transcendence in all things. It was impossible to deny that God orchestrated these things. They had received the Holy Ghost just as Peter and the others had on the Day of Pentecost.

Peter's actions created a problem for some of the brethren. They discussed the matter with great intensity, sparks flew as we would say, and not everyone was happy about Peter's report or actions. In Acts 15:10, Peter inquired of the council: "Now therefore why tempt ye God, to put a yoke upon the neck of the disciples, which neither our fathers nor we were able to bear?" First, God cannot be tempted by human issues. When we attempt to tempt God, we try to persuade Him to do something inconsistent with His nature.

Some leaders were trying to mix the old order with the new. They were dragging the old cultural ceremonies from the Law into the economy of Grace. Yes, they were carrying the dead. It is costly and exasperating to hang on to that which is dead. It is a heavy burden that should be laid to rest. If we continue to carry around dead things, they will corrupt the new. The dead things of yesterday are meant to be laid aside so that new ways might be embraced.

Peter's words could be said like this: "Listen, brothers, we are attempting to bring something from the old order that was nothing more than a yoke of bondage for us and our fathers!

We should not repeat this. Let's not do this to the new disciples."

A disciple is someone learning the ways of Christ. The apostles and elders had to settle this quickly because the Pharisees wanted them discipled in the Law of Moses, along with being circumcised in the flesh. Neither of those things represents whether one has come into Christ. They are remnants of what was once the move of God.

Like these early leaders, there are some disagreements we must be willing to work our way through for the good of the Kingdom. Paul wrote a clear message about these matters later.

> Stand fast therefore in the liberty wherewith Christ hath made us free, and be not entangled again with the yoke of bondage. Behold, I Paul say unto you, that if ye be circumcised, Christ shall profit you nothing. For I testify again to every man that is circumcised, that he is a debtor to do the whole Law. Christ is become of no effect unto you, whosoever of you are justified by the Law; ye are fallen from grace. (Galatians 5:1–4)

This is a powerful statement. Without the spirit of revelation, it is difficult to understand how powerful this was in a first-century context and setting. He established that if one committed to circumcision, that person committed to keeping the entire Law. All must be accepted if any element is taken up from the Law. In doing so, Christ has become of no effect to that person. Paul finally said that whoever believes they are justified by the Law has fallen from grace. Have you heard people argue over whether it is possible to fall from grace? The Holy Scripture states it is possible.

> For it is impossible for those who were once enlightened, and have tasted of the heavenly gift, and were made partakers of the Holy Ghost, and have tasted the good word of God, and the powers of the world to come, if they shall fall away, to renew them again unto repentance; seeing they crucify to themselves the Son of God afresh and put him to an open shame. (Hebrews 6:4–6)

Even today, people are often terrorized after reading the passages above because they don't know the original context; the enemy takes advantage of their ignorance. The missing key to understanding this passage is not knowing how much pressure the Hebrew believers experienced.

Daily, they faced the decision to continue in Christ or go back under the Law. If they went back, they would deny the work of the cross because it became the foundation of separation between the old and the new. *The power and energy of grace are denied when one returns to the law*. A person could do only one of two things: Move forward in grace or go back in perdition under the law.

Many years ago, this was a heaven and hell issue. If someone had fallen from grace momentarily, messed up, and walked away, it was taught that this was a permanent condition. It left people afraid to die because they thought they would be in hell forever. The teaching back then said, "That's it for you! You have crucified Christ afresh!" Some of you may remember this. I know it might be like I'm speaking Greek to most of the younger ones.

I remember how difficult this was for struggling saints. Different ones have called me and asked if they could ever be saved again because of their committed infraction. My answer was, "Yes!" The apostle John tells us, "If we confess our sins, he is faithful and just to forgive us our sins, and to cleanse us from all unrighteousness" (1 John 1:9). Confession and forgiveness works far beynd the new birth experience. Saints will experience the love and mercy of God throughout their lives.

The book's writer spoke to Hebrew people. They understood the Law and the Tabernacle. They knew about the sacrifices. They understood those things. The Hebrews equally understood that none of that ever changed them. But Jesus brought an end to that order. As Paul says in Romans 10:4, "For Christ is the end of the law for righteousness to every one that believeth." Christ came to earth to end that system and establish the grace economy. Hallelujah!

One of the most powerful truths of the grace economy is that we all get to know God from the least to the greatest of us. No single person must know God through another's relationship with God. The New Covenant brought us into global equalization and a new normal which the dispensation of grace had released. Now, everybody can choose to get to know Him. But these Hebrew believers were on the edge of drifting back into legalism—it was familiar ground for the Hebrews. Paul called those teachers (those releasing something other than the gospel of grace) "the concision" (Philippians 3:2). That means *the mutilators[13]*. He warned believers to stay away from them.

Most of these teachers were from the Pharisaical ranks. They demanded that brethren be circumcised in the flesh to be saved. This was a mutilation of the truth. Then and now, when God's people are under the pressure of such teachings, they become worn out. Not even one of those teachings had any validity for the New Covenant.

God loves us, and we are acceptable to Him because of Christ. We make progress in God's Kingdom because of Christ. He opened every necessary door for us. So, if someone fell into legalism, or embraced the Law economy again, repent! Come back to the cross and refocus on Jesus' death, burial, and resurrection. And when a person does, they will find the statement of the finished work of Christ. That statement is our freedom and evidence of the finished work. From time to time, we need a fresh view of Him. Hallelujah! He's the one who died for us and loved us that much. Christ died for us while we were sinners and completely messed up.

I challenge us to get a new fresh view of that. As my wife says, "I am over and above! I am over what is past, and I am above going back!" Nothing about the Law economy will be attractive to us when we possess this. Returning to the old order was a dangling carrot to the Hebrew people. The writer wanted them to understand that's not what you want to chase.

Stay on the victorious side of the cross. Stay enlightened! Continue to drink of the good Holy Ghost! Keep your connection with the powers of the age to come. Stay on the side of the One who finished it all for us. The question concerning your eternal security will not plague you when you do this. The first-century church had to work these things out.

The apostles called those alternative views *yokes of bondage.* So, in our new view, what should we be getting? Remember, we're talking about *The Savior's Perfect Yoke.* We should see nothing but completeness in Christ. He stands in the gap between the two ages. Look unto Him! The view before Christ is nothing more than the arm of the flesh displayed. We can spend an entire year seeing Him or being mesmerized by the flesh. It is up to each of us. I'm encouraging us to be awakened to Christ. I'll ask you this question: "Are you awake?"

Each person still has an assignment. God didn't change his mind. Are you awake? It reminds me of Paul as he writes the letter to the Ephesians. The first portion of the book (chapters 1–3) is a powerful theological statement. Beginning with chapter 4, he tells us how to walk based on what was taught in the first three chapters.

Paul first said (in Ephesians 4:1), "Walk worthy!" We are to walk worthy of our vocation. The idea is to walk like you normally would because of knowing who you are in Christ. Afterward, he says in Ephesians 4:17 (NKJV), "You should no longer walk as the rest of the Gentiles walk, in the futility of their mind." It is the same today. The unrenewed, unsaved, un-regenerated walk (in the lust of their flesh, the lust of the eyes, and the pride of life) is not the way you are walk in life.

In 1 Corinthians 4:16 and 1 Corinthians 11:1, Paul says, "Imitate me," which means to *mimic* me. He declared he was imitating Christ. This speaks to his extraordinary confidence. Paul was very clear about his actions synchronizing with Christ's actions. In Ephesians 2, he spoke of how Christ loved us and sacrificed Himself unconditionally on our behalf. Paul was showing them the life of Christ in his saying, "That's how we should walk."

And then later, in Ephesians 5:8 (NKJV), he says, "You were once darkness, but now you are light in the Lord. Walk as children of light." Ephesians 5:9 continues to state that the light radiating from us is in all goodness and the fruit of the Spirit.

The final thing Paul said was (jumping forward to Ephesians 5:15), "walk circumspectly." That means *walking with accuracy*. The season we are currently living in demands accuracy. Are you ready for me to dig a little deeper? Because of inaccuracy, there will be closures of churches that are just barely existing. They are living in another season and failing to walk circumspectly. If you are destined to be a world-changer, you can't just exist. That is not in your spiritual DNA. Remember what I said to you? You are coded with God's DNA for finishing, not failing.

In between walking as light and walking accurately, Paul commands us to be awake and arise. We awake in a new consciousness and arise in a new dimension of resurrection. **You**

are not going to get up until you wake up. Christ shines in us and gives us light *as we arise.* Light in this context is understanding. We could see it as a new strategy. However, you must wake up first.

Take this book series, for instance, and the God's Kingdom Leaders' Summits. Why are we drawn to higher-level studies, teaching series, leaders' conferences with teachings like these? *Because we begin to hear something from the Spirit that commands us to wake up.* No one can afford to sleep spiritually in this hour. When one is awake, one is ready for action. You're ready for Christ to drop that yoke of bondage off you, ease the perfect yoke on your neck, and place the light burden on your back. That's when your steps will be ignited for the new season, and you will *stir up the gift* inside. (And we will delve deep into that instruction to *Stir Up the Gift* in the next book in this series from our God's Kingdom Leaders' summits.) For now, let's continue to lean into *The Savior's Perfect Yoke!*

Submission makes love easy and enjoyable.
Love gives birth to willful and cheerful submission.
Where there is love and submission is missing, and
where there is submission and love is missing,
the result is that the other becomes
a burden and a uneasy yoke.
— Paul Bamikole

CHAPTER NINE

AN EASY YOKE, A LIGHT BURDEN

And I will make them and the places round about my hill a blessing; and I will cause the shower to come down in his season; there shall be showers of blessing. And the tree of the field shall yield her fruit, and the earth shall yield her increase, and they shall be safe in their land, and shall know that I am the LORD, when I have broken the bands of their yoke, and delivered them out of the hand of those that served themselves of them.

Ezekiel 34:26–27

When Isaac spoke to Esau about the yoke being broken off his neck, there was a clear picture of where the yoke was placed. You should think about the neck when you hear the word *yoke*. I explained previously that the neck speaks of the will of man. Jesus, in the invitation, said with that imagery, "I'm going to place a new yoke [on your will], and it's going to be easy. The burden it creates is light."

Let's look at a few more pictures from the Old Testament about this. The Lord referred to the Egyptian bondage as a yoke. See this in Leviticus 26:13: "I am the LORD your God, which brought you forth out of the land of Egypt, that ye should not be their bondmen; and I have broken the bands of your yoke, and made you go upright."

In examining this more closely, I want us to consider the ministry of Moses, Aaron, and Miriam. Why am I saying that and not just Moses? For a very specific reason. It is all part of *The Savior's Perfect Yoke*. When the prophets considered this, they didn't see one walking alone. They saw Moses, Aaron, and Miriam. What does that tell you about God? A threefold cord cannot easily be broken. Even when Miriam displeased the LORD, it distressed the whole camp of Israel. But look at what happened. Israel's progress halted until that portion of the yoke was restored. They had to wait for her restoration. I greatly respect the ministry of Moses, but it was not Moses alone that delivered them. It was not an all-boys club.

Anytime God births something, whether a person or an idea, every portion of the yoke must be in place. It must carry both the male and female expressions of God.

We will dive deeper into the Word in future God's Kingdom Leaders' Summits and our third book in this series, *What God Has Joined*. For now, I'd like to ask how many of you remember the word *zygote* from biology? The word zygote is

108

from the Greek word *zygos* (or *zugos)* which we introduced in chapter one.

Quoting from our text in chapter one, from "the phrase, 'Take my yoke' (Matthew 11:29), the word *yoke* is engaging because it is the Greek word **zygos**[14] (pronounced 'zugos'). And the idea that it conveys is **to be joined.**" Similarly, a zygote is formed when the sperm cell hooks up with the ovum. **Together, they form a yoke.** That yoke becomes a person. It is nonsense to think otherwise. Some people call the zygote tissue and refuse to call it a person. However, we cannot deny that every person born into this earth started as a human zygote. Everyone's physical existence starts as a yoke.

As I read Leviticus, I see God bringing forth free men rather than bondmen. He made it clear that He had *broken the bands of the previous yoke* (Isaiah 58:6). That piqued my interest. What would the **bands** of a yoke be? Of course, I studied the word **bands**. It meant the U-shaped apparatus in the yoke that you place about the neck. It was connected by a beam that holds the U-shapes (the bands or bonds) together. Do you get the picture?

There is another way to describe this. The U-shape portion is called an **oxbow**[15]. I find that rather unique. In my study, the Lord said they had that on their necks. Father God declared it was broken, and He had made them go upright in that breaking off. Oh, hallelujah.

It is equally interesting that in geography, an oxbow is also the S-shape created by a river as the water flows. How does this happen? A river flows and then takes or makes a path different from its normal course. It makes a shape best called an oxbow. Well, the river will find the straightest or easiest course of flow. This action creates the oxbow. Normally, an oxbow holds water, but it's not very vibrant. The oxbow becomes the evidence that the river once ran here.

Let's apply that to our journey in life. The river in our illustration is the Spirit of God. An oxbow indicates that this was once a place of abundant activity by God's Spirit. An oxbow also tells us that there were rich deposits of God's life. They have been traded for the traditions of men. Jesus said that these traditions of men make the commandment of God of no effect. If you want *to neutralize* God's activity in your life, just create an oxbow—an alternate path. If you want to *be neutralized*, just go ahead with the choices that get you back into a U-shape of a yoke you are not supposed to be in! That is not His will for your lives, but he will allow you to choose.

I hear the body of Christ repeatedly crying out to be released from the oxbows we have entered. They are lifeless—one will not find God's purposes in these oxbows. No one will feel His power, presence, or provision there. In other words, you feel something much deeper in your bones, in your heart, but you think that you don't know how to break out.

Well, the scripture speaks of a river whose streams shall make glad the city of God (Psalm 46:4). One of the first things Jesus called us was a city. Hallelujah! As a city, the corporate Body of Christ, we will be gloriously affected *by a river;* we will not have that same result in an oxbow. If a correction isn't made, the oxbow becomes a swamp.

Let's talk about the swamp. A swamp contains water, but the water isn't beneficial for people. There are no controls on the water in the swamps. Rivers are quite different. A river has borders and banks that control the flow of water. A swamp doesn't have a *water flow;* it is a stagnant breeding ground for all that decays.

Too many get cut-off from living water because they position themselves to be influenced by something other than the river of God. You see, without the movement of waters from the flow of the river, the stagnant waters can be a haven for opportunistic, deadly creatures. They are laying in wait for their moment to take advantage of the prey. Don't be easy prey because you are in the waters that *used to be* a part of the river; don't be caught in the swamp that formed when the river changed course! Tell yourself, "Stay out of the swamp." Go ahead and speak that out!

Now let's talk more about the river. Like natural rivers, the river of God has many streams of expression, not just one. For instance, Israel was twelve tribes, not just one. They would find their greatest joy in flowing with and respecting one another. Every tribe was a stream. The experience of the streams release joy in the hearts of those who partake of the river. It brings to remembrance all the good things of God.

A powerful example of a river with many streams flowing into it is the Mississippi River in the United States of America. It has five major tributaries—the Arkansas, Illinois, Missouri, Ohio, and Red rivers. They all help to make the Mississippi River system what it is. The various expressions and streams in the body of Christ serve the same purpose. They each reveal something of the goodness of God, and also how God chooses to manifest Himself in the human experience. It is His purpose that every stream and every tributary make a contribution without becoming a carbon copy of another. With this system intact, we get to appreciate the multi-faceted wisdom of God.

Let's put this in context. Rejoining our earlier discussion, where was Israel at that moment? Consider when the book of Deuteronomy was written. They were forty years into their journey. It was forty years earlier when they first came out of Egypt, as recorded in Exodus. Miriam and the ladies picked up tambourines and danced with great joy. The yoke of Egypt had been broken off them.

Many things happened over the next forty years. God expected that Israel would be a thankful, obedient people. Unfortunately, they spent an inordinate amount of time in rebellion, or in thinking of ways to rebel. For one, they had the uprising of Korah, Dathan, Abiram, and their company recorded in Numbers chapter 16. Incidents like that indicated they were no longer serving the Lord with a joyful heart. Carnality overtook them! The children of Israel watched the earth swallow them in an earthquake that didn't affect anyone else. They watched many of their brethren ask for flesh because they didn't like manna. God gave them flesh until it came out of their noses (Numbers 11:18-20).

Moses watched vicious serpents bite the people who complained against the way God was leading them (Numbers 21:4-9). God knows the number of times they picked up stones ready to stone Moses. There were occasions Israel wanted to choose a leader to escort them back to Egypt.

Father God had warned the children of Israel about disobedience as they prepared to go into the promised land. Note below what God said to them if they chose not to serve the Lord with joyfulness and gladness of heart for the abundance of all things. What a way to introduce His expectation to them!

> Because thou servedst not the LORD thy God with joyfulness, and with gladness of heart, for the abundance of all things; therefore shalt thou serve thine enemies which the LORD shall send against thee, in hunger, and in thirst, and in nakedness, and in want of all things: and he shall put a yoke of iron upon thy neck until he have destroyed thee. (Deuteronomy 28:47–48)

These and many more incidents were sandwiched between their initial deliverance and this moment forty years later. After the great and terrible wilderness experience, the ones left alive had forgotten the thankfulness of the first generation. So, the Lord told the next generation to serve Him with gladness.

He was teaching them to keep drinking from the river of joy. "Keep singing! Declare that I'm good!" He was teaching them how to keep the wrong yoke off their necks. In the abundance of good things, there wasn't a feeble one among them for forty years! They were fed every day for forty years, and their thirst was quenched for forty years in a hostile environment.

They couldn't wear their clothes out! Israel kept their shoes for forty years. God terrorized the tribes of people around them to prevent them from attacking His people for forty years. Father God shielded them and prevented attacks on them for forty years.

Think about all the abundance of God's goodness to them. These things happened to at least three million people. One of the major accomplishments was God's ability to keep them disease-free. None of that! There are no viral outbreaks, plagues, or desert diseases because of constant exposure to the desert. It is alarming how they chose to speak to God with ungrateful hearts.

But realize… they are a picture of humanity's continued behavior! We are often "they." We must remember these things. When you think about all the goodness God has given us, we should constantly shout for joy.

God was telling second-generation Israel that *their inheritance was in view.* Don't be like the first generation. They refused to serve the Lord their God with joyfulness, with gladness of heart, for the abundance of all the things. Therefore, they bowed and served enemies that the Lord sent against them. This list included the basic things a son of God should expect just by being a son. The LORD said their lack would put a yoke of iron upon their necks until they were destroyed.

Why was this warning necessary for the new generation? *It was because of the example of the previous generation. It would be easy to follow their example if not watchful, purposeful, and intentional.* Their elders had been murmurers and complainers, always questioning God. They had been willfully disobedient to God's instruction. That was the example the new generation had before them. And it is still before us in the world today.

Many years later, Paul writes about this and admonishes us not to follow that first generation example:

> But with many of them God was not well pleased: for they were overthrown in the wilderness. Now these things were our examples, to the intent we should not lust after evil things, as they also lusted. Neither be ye idolaters, as were some of them; as it is written, The people sat down to eat and drink, and rose up to play. Neither let us commit fornication, as some of them committed, and fell in one day three and twenty thousand. Neither let us tempt Christ, as some of them also tempted, and were destroyed of serpents. Neither murmur ye, as some of them also murmured, and were destroyed of the destroyer.
>
> Now all these things happened unto them for examples: and they are written for our admonition, upon whom the ends of the world are come. (1 Corinthians 10:5–11)

Another model to consider was Israel's first three kings—Saul, David, and Solomon. Each of them reigned for forty years. So, you have the full scope of 120 years. The number 120 in scripture speaks of the *end of all flesh*. By the time Solomon's reign concluded, we should see a booming kingdom without the flesh order in control. The kingdom should be set up for advancement, particularly when the 120 mark is reached.

I deal with the principle of 120 and the *end of all flesh* further in other teachings, but right now I want you to see this: Saul became king because of Israel's desire to be like the other nations. Based upon the prophetic words over the tribes, it was a mistake to anoint him. First, he was not from the right tribe. Saul was from the tribe of Benjamin. The prophetic word said kings would come out of Judah (Genesis 49:8-12; 1 Chronicles 5:2; Psalm 78:67-72). We can see that word come to pass, starting with David. That's why Caleb had to outlive Joshua because he was from the tribe of Judah. In contrast, Joshua was from the tribe of Ephraim, who was the son of Joseph. This was a divine setup to get the kingly tribe positioned.

Joshua was in the middle when considering the first three leaders of Israel after their Egyptian bondage—Moses, Joshua, and Caleb. He carried a marketplace anointing. His assignment was to make sure that all the tribes received their inheritance. Caleb lived much longer than Joshua. God was placing this visual before us. Real rulership was going to come out of Judah. So, the question came up at the beginning of the book of Judges chapter 1: "*Whom do we send first?*" God immediately said, "*Send Judah first!*" (vv. 1-2).

This wasn't unusual. When the tribes were marching, Judah was leading. When the tribes were settled around the Tabernacle, Judah was placed first on the eastern side. This was the entrance side of the Tabernacle. Yes, it was right to send Judah first.

Judah was wise enough to speak to his brother, Simeon, to go in with him. **It is always good to yoke the apostolic and prophetic together** although this particular scenario was typology. The order is first apostles and second prophets. Simeon's name derives its meaning from the Hebrew root word *šāma* which means "*hearing with an intent to obey*[16]." Hearing from God is the nature of the prophetic. (Actually it should be the common ground for all of God's people.) Judah and Simeon became yoked together. You could say that just as Barnabas and Saul were yoked to *the work*, so were Judah and Simeon.

Let's return for a moment and deal with the yoke between Saul and the children of Israel. In studying throughout 1 Samuel, a king (Saul) was the people's desire. They wanted a king who would go out and come in before them. *It is important to note that Israel was rejecting God as their King by doing this* (1 Samuel 10:19). The prophet Samuel tried to counsel them against that decision. Summarizing to full context from 1 Samuel 8, the people said, "Oh yes, that is exactly what we want! We want a king like everybody else." God commanded the prophet to give them what they wanted but tell them what their king would be like. Saul was known as the people's king.

Continuing through the text of 1 Samuel 8 you will see that Samuel gave the people advance notice of Saul's disposition. He could have easily said, "Don't be disappointed when you see what he's like. He's going to take your land. He's going to take your sons and your daughters. He's going to take your money." If you read through that list, it shows us that Saul is *a taker*. He's covetous. "Israel, your king, is just like you." We can gather from the context that God told them, in a sense, "He's *your mirror* for the next forty years. You will be ready for *my mirror* when that period is over."

David, a man after God's heart, was from the right tribe, Judah. Was he perfect in character? Of course, the answer is no. But there was something about his heart that pleased God. He was willing to do God's will. In 2 Samuel 7:8, the Lord says, "Now therefore so shalt thou say unto my servant David, 'Thus saith the LORD of hosts, "I took thee from the sheepcote, from following the sheep, to be ruler over my people, over Israel."'" Notice that David was among the sheep. Saul was chasing donkeys (1 Samuel 9) when he was selected. One man was with sheep and the other donkeys. That's a big difference. Wow!

God also said David would rule by the integrity of his heart and the skillfulness of his hands (Psalm 78:72; paraphrased). Notice what was first. It wasn't the skill we see in his hands or his natural ability. There was that something called integrity or wholeness in his heart, hallelujah! The skillfulness of his hands sprung out of the integrity of his heart. Integrity should always be the first consideration in choosing a leader. If one is highly skilled, that is a plus; however, integrity should be first on the list.

God essentially said, "That's my man." The Lord placed David's enemies under his feet. That's why Jesus was likened to Abraham and David more than any other men in the Old

Testament. God put all of Jesus' enemies under His feet. When David handed the kingdom to Solomon, there were no enemies left. Things were prepared for Solomon to be successful. He was assigned to build God a house worthy to live in. This house wasn't a tent or something temporary. It was constructed of stones, implying its permanence.

Solomon built God a house; however, he made several critical personal mistakes. God had forewarned him not to do three things. Like many, it is the Genesis 3 violation all over again—Solomon ignored the direct instruction of the Lord. Solomon multiplied gold, wives, and horses. God had spoken to him never to do this. But even further, he did something that made it difficult for his son, Rehoboam, to succeed. Solomon orchestrated a heavy taxation program to support his other building projects. He taxed the people repeatedly. After his death, the congregation of Israel came to King Rehoboam for relief.

> Thy father made our yoke grievous: now therefore make thou the grievous service of thy father, and his heavy yoke which he put upon us, lighter, and we will serve thee. (1 Kings 12:4)

The people weren't seeking to be irresponsible; they just needed some mercy. Rehoboam asked the elders for counsel. He wanted to know what would make him an effective leader.

> And King Rehoboam consulted with the old men, that stood before Solomon his father

while he yet lived, and said, "How do ye advise that I may answer this people?" And they spake unto him, saying, "If thou wilt be a servant unto this people this day, and wilt serve them, and answer them, and speak good words to them, then they will be thy servants forever." (1 Kings 12:6–7)

Israel asked Rehoboam for the same thing Jesus offered men when He invited them to come unto Him (Matthew 11:30), "My yoke is easy, and My burden is light!" They needed and desired a leader that would do justly, love mercy, and walk humbly with God (Micah 6:8; paraphrased).

Again, the issue was the heavy burden of taxation. It was within Rehoboam's power to make it lighter. If he had listened to the counsel of the elders, he would have precisely done that. First Kings 12:8 tells us however that "he forsook the counsel of the old men, which they had given him, and consulted with the young men that were grown up with him, and which stood before him." The counsel of the younger men led to the division of the nation. It was not wise counsel. When people are encircled by pressure, they don't need the answer Rehoboam gave them.

My father made your yoke heavy, and I will add to your yoke: my father also chastised you with whips, but I will chastise you with scorpions. (1 Kings 12:14)

This is a powerful example for us today as we train generations to walk and to lead with Godly wisdom. The key is being led by Holy Spirit. For example, generally, I love the idea of progressive thinking in younger men and women. They often add vibrancy and life with fresh expression. However, when I need solid counsel, that's another situation. I will seek the wisdom of more mature and proven saints. They will give you what you need to hear, not what you want to hear.

In Rehoboam's case, the nation's progression was standing in the balance. We see this every year with many churches in transition. As a new leader, the people will connect with you, or they will leave you. For the new king, making their yoke heavier was not the wisest thing to do. Following the counsel of the seniors would have been the best move to make. If Rehoboam had complied, the congregation would have followed him forever. He chose to do his own thing and cater to the approval of the younger, exuberant but unseasoned counsel.

Now, for the rest of the story. Ten tribes, ready to follow King Rehoboam, separated from him. They were initially ready to follow him for life. All he had to do was to make their yoke lighter. He listened to the wrong counsel. A portion of this was a divine setup. The prophet, Ahijah, had spoken the LORD'S counsel on the matter before this event.

We see that there are two things at work: divine sovereignty and human stubbornness. I'm glad the King of kings has lightened our loads and soothed us with grace. That is always our pattern. The pattern of God's Kingdom is God's way of handling things. We can continue our journey knowing that we have an easy yoke. This brings me back to our opening scripture in this chapter:

> And I will make them and the places round about my hill a blessing; and I will cause the shower to come down in his season; there shall be showers of blessing. And the tree of the field shall yield her fruit, and the earth shall yield her increase, and they shall be safe in their land, and shall know that I am the LORD, when I have broken the bands of their yoke, and delivered them out of the hand of those that served themselves of them. (Ezekiel 34:26–27)

These verses above beautifully portray living with an easy yoke. It is a life of increase and fruitfulness. It is a life of safety and protection. It is the kingdom of God in manifestation on earth.

> Only the man who follows the command of Jesus single-mindedly, and unresistingly lets his yoke rest upon him, finds his burden easy, and under its gentle pressure receives the power to persevere in the right way. The command of Jesus is hard, unutterably hard, for those who try to resist it. But for those who willingly submit, the yoke is easy, and the burden is light.
> — Dietrich Bonhoeffer, The Cost of Discipleship

CHAPTER TEN

TRADING YOKES

And he was withdrawn from them about a stone's
cast, and kneeled down, and prayed, saying,
"Father, if thou be willing, remove this cup from me:
nevertheless not my will, but thine, be done".
Luke 22:41–42

Earlier, I introduced the *law of first use* from the book of Genesis. When I study a term, I like to plumb the depths of that word. One of the ways to get it is to go back and utilize that law of first use. Then, I trace it through the scriptures.

Something that I want to warn you of, and I think it is important, is that we should not practice isolating scriptural verses in our studies. Make sure you study the texts and the context in which your focus word is used. Otherwise, you could come up with heretical conclusions.

I will give you an example. Some years ago, an individual was studying the scriptures to understand the idea of life and breath. The passage he studied (Psalm 104:24–30) had **nothing to do with humans.** It was about the lower creation—the beasts of the sea. The psalmist stated, "You take away their breath, they die and return to their dust" (v. 29). Because this person isolated the scriptures in his studies, he made a contextual error. He applied what he read (in a very limited glimpse) to humans rather than the true context—sea creatures and animals. He said, "Once you're dead, you're dead! There's nothing else to a person's life once death occurs." There was no changing of his mind. (But I did and do now insert the question, "What then are you going to do with the scriptures teaching on the resurrection of the dead?") He could have only drawn that conclusion by isolating the scriptures.

So what am I saying to us now? *Don't do that.* There are proven ways to avoid improper interpretations. First, look at the historical context and setting. Second, consider what God is saying at that moment. Third, look at the prophetic and eternal significance. How does a scripture apply as you move from one generation to the next without deleting any hermeneutical principles? These are vital points for every believer, and they are especially important for every teacher and minister! You'll miss a lot if you're just looking for the prophetic alone. And, if you're only looking for history, you will equally miss a lot. You must consider the historical, current, and eternal.

As I studied the word *yoke*, I made the historical and prophetic application. The first use of the word *yoke* occurs in Genesis 27:38. It is used in the tangle of Esau and Jacob. Isaac, their father, and Rebecca, their mother, were highly involved in this situation.

Let's review the story. Esau and Jacob were twins. Isaac favored Esau, and Rebecca favored Jacob. So, the parents contributed to their sibling rivalry. Still, even so, God had spoken about these boys long before this event. God said, "The elder shall serve the younger" (Genesis 25:23). In this case, Esau would serve Jacob (Genesis 25:25–26). We must learn, remember, and hold fast to the truth that the word of God trumps all our parental desires.

The scripture reveals that the struggle began with the boys in the womb. In the transition process, Jacob reached and grabbed Esau's heel. That's where the name Jacob came from—he was a heel snatcher. Eventually, Jacob was known as a trickster, schemer, and conniver. That was his character, but it wasn't to be permanent. It was for the moment. What is the lesson in this? We don't have to lock anyone into a certain perception perpetually. It is never that way—**God works in that person's life over the entire lifetime**. He's still orchestrating some things. God can turn anyone. The Bible tells us that the king's heart is in the hands of the Lord.

In due time, God turned Jacob. But in the Genesis narrative, Esau had come back from the field. He was hungry. Jacob would not feed Esau unless he released his birthright to him. Esau sold the birthright for a bowl of beans. Esau felt he was starving. He lightly esteemed the birthright, thinking, "what good is a birthright to a starving man?" So, he sold it.

Esau didn't seem too concerned about not having birthright privileges anymore. The firstborn son received two things from his father: the birthright and the blessing. It was also a double portion of responsibility. What (later) concerned Esau? It was the blessing! In those days, a father would draw in a son or daughter and speak words of affirmation over them. Those words helped them to navigate their path in life. The father would not rescind those words. We see the same behavior in our Heavenly Father when He blessed Adam and spoke over him. I see a general rule in this: A father cannot bless without saying words. When we, as sons, bless our Heavenly Father, we may kneel or raise our hands; nevertheless, words accompany those actions because you can't bless without them.

Isaac was aging, and he wanted to discharge his duties. Rebecca knew he wanted to do that. Come on and walk through the story in Genesis with me. Because she favored Jacob, she prepared him to receive the blessing. At the same time, Isaac had instructed Esau to go into the field and prepare meat for him. Once Isaac consumed it, he would bless him.

This is where the story gets interesting, and we also see the carnality of human conniving. Jacob had already engineered the birthright from Esau. Now, he's about to steal the blessing from him as well. Rebecca prepared Jacob to go before his father and receive the blessing. Once everything was in place, he did exactly that. Although Isaac sensed something might be wrong, he gave the blessing anyway; thinking he was speaking over Esau, he spoke. But it was Jacob who was present to receive it. Now, Jacob has the birthright and the blessing.

In the meantime, Esau came from the field with his meat prepared. Jacob had barely gone from Isaac's presence. Esau was ready to receive the blessing when Isaac informed him that he had given the blessing and so Jacob would be blessed. Isaac even made Jacob to be Esau's master. "And Esau said unto his father, 'Hast thou but one blessing, my father? Bless me, even me also, O my father'" (Genesis 27:38). Esau wept over the blessing, but not over the birthright. He realized he had lost it all. The remorse of losing everything drove his response.

Isaac spoke these words over Esau. You could see his compassionate heart for his firstborn in his words:

> Isaac, his father, answered and said unto him, "Behold, thy dwelling shall be the fatness of the earth, and of the dew of heaven from above; and by the sword shalt thou live, and shalt serve thy brother; and it shall come to pass when thou shalt have the dominion, that thou shalt break his yoke from off thy neck." (Genesis 27:39–40)

Although this was not the smoothest transaction, things are in place for the elder to serve the younger. When we hear a word from God in the earthly realm, it has been finished in the heavens from the beginning. For example, the story of Esau and Jacob is a powerful visual of the old nature succumbing to the new. Another example is that God showed Daniel battles in the heavens that were precursors to events in future times. God painted this picture for us in these characters regarding the purpose of the Kingdom.

Isaac told Esau that Esau's submission to Jacob would have an end. Also, Isaac tells him there's a different path for him in the future. The yoke Esau was wearing would change, and he would move into a position of dominion. But for the moment, Jacob's yoke on him was heavy.

Consider this: The yoke we get from culture, and maybe even from church, can be just as heavy and taxing. But Jesus said, "I'm giving you an easy yoke and a light burden." What makes it that way? The Lord's dealings will have changed and adjusted our perspective on things. We wake up one day, and the same thing suddenly looks different. However, the yoke is still a yoke, and the burden is still a burden.

Like Paul, *God's grace gives us a different outlook on suffering*. It enables us to admit that something may be difficult. Still, it's not overwhelming to the degree that we're considering quitting. Part of our learning is to shift how we perceive things, how we learn to reframe our experience to agree with God's eternal perspective. Will you choose to agree with God? Even if it means releasing your offense, grief, or independence?

Another truth in this story is that **our previous season will serve our new season.** The elder serves the younger. That has always been the plan of God. Our generation must serve the coming generations **by transmitting the things we're receiving from God to the next generation.** They will be responsible for utilizing those transmissions and building effectively with them.

Esau did not break Jacob's yoke through anger or the sword. It happened through the change in Jacob's life in Genesis 32. While God was working in Jacob, He was also working in Esau. The work had to be done in Jacob first because he carried the right of the firstborn. The responsibility to be a benefactor to others comes with having the birthright and the blessing. A father would give the firstborn son a double portion of the family's inheritance. Still, he was equally responsible for taking care of his younger siblings.

Remember the case of Elijah and Elisha? Elisha wanted a double portion of Elijah's spirit. He was saying, "I'm your first-born prophetic son!" *That was the only thing that legally qualified him for a double portion.* **Yet he had to be continually present and faithful in the transition to receive it.**

So, Jacob had the double portion, and Esau walked momentarily with a yoke. Notice where the yoke was? It was on his neck. You do the same with oxen. If you're going to plow with them and manage them, you must place a yoke on their neck. This means that oxen serve best when they are under a yoke. The same is true for us. We serve best with the Lord's easy yoke and light burden.

God called Israel stiff-necked on various occasions. What was He speaking about? Their (and our) willingness to live rebelliously. Contrariwise, a willingness to submit enables Him to direct our steps much more effectively. And, when we bow to him this way, He will never refer to us as *stiff-necked*.

Because I knew that thou art obstinate, and thy neck is an iron sinew, thy brow brass; I have even from the beginning declared it to thee; before it came to pass I shewed it thee: lest thou shouldest say, "mine idol hath done them, and my graven image, and my molten image, hath commanded them." (Isaiah 48:4–5)

But they obeyed not, neither inclined their ear, but made their neck stiff, that they might not hear, nor receive instruction. (Jeremiah 17:23)

Yet the LORD testified against Israel, and against Judah, by all the prophets, and by all the seers, saying, "Turn ye from your evil ways, and keep my commandments and my statutes, according to all the law which I commanded your fathers, and which I sent to you by my servants the prophets." Notwithstanding, they would not hear, but hardened their necks, like to the neck of their fathers, that did not believe in the LORD their God. (2 Kings 17:13–14)

God wasn't speaking of their neck being physically frozen or immovable. God spoke of their will resisting His will, and that's a violation. The Lord describes this condition as stiff-necked. So, when you look at the word *neck*, it may figuratively speak of your will. (Although we always note that the spiritual condition can cause the physical body to respond by exhibiting a similar condition. The body does not lie; it responds to the spirit.) How do we know that Jesus was not stiff-necked? Again, we have the scripture to vouch for Him:

> Then said Jesus unto them, "When ye have lifted up the Son of man, then shall ye know that I am he and that I do nothing of myself; but as my Father hath taught me, I speak these things. And He that sent me is with me: the Father hath not left me alone; for I do always those things that please him." (John 8:28–29)

What an incredible statement! Generally, the last thing any of us releases is the human will. If God asks us to do something, the first inclination of the natural man is to work it out intellectually. Second, we must determine in our hearts that it is for the greater good of the Kingdom. That is an emotional decision. In these, two expressions of the soul have engaged— the intellect and emotions. *The will* must then become yoked with the intellect and emotions to form a threefold cord. This is either a decision to be in agreement or disagreement with the will of God. Let it be our purposeful decision to respond, spirit, soul (mind, will, emotions), and body (action), like Jesus, and say, "Not my will but Thine be done."

The Heavenly Father wants us to comply with His will *willingly.* **That is the highest form of giving to God when I'm willing to do God's will** *without any alterations.* We have traded yokes as we do. Yes, we have traded for Jesus' easy yoke. Hallelujah!

When Jesus prayed in the Garden of Gethsemane, He modeled compliance for us. He finalized yielding His will to the Heavenly Father. Jesus had set his face like flint to go toward Jerusalem. Jesus knew that this was the final place where all the eternal conclusions would windup. He would not be distracted even by "ministry opportunities" because He was determined to finish what the Father had tasked (sent) Him to do.

The time had come. The final night before Jesus's crucifixion was one of preparation for His disciples. Amazing things were spoken during the last supper. He prepared them for a new normal. The old normal had an expiration date affixed to it. They had to have a better understanding of their new mission. The Gospel of John gives us a fuller view of this conversation that lasted several hours after Judas left the room.

After more than fifty years in ministry now, I want to give some practical counsel to senior leaders right now. If someone has determined to leave you, let them go! Now, I'm not calling them Judas; I'm not saying they will betray you. If you attempt to hold them, you're wasting time. It's impossible to hold someone who doesn't want to be with you. Jesus began the conversation in John 13:31 with that understanding. It did not conclude until he finished praying in John 17. Afterward, He was ready to finish His assignment.

The disciples were burdened by what they were hearing. They wanted to reject Jesus' discourse rather than receive it as a new normal. Jesus spoke of how He had glorified the Heavenly

Father. He glorified Him by finishing the work given to Him. He didn't run the race halfway and quit; no, He finished. Jesus would turn the extension of the Kingdom over to His disciples. His example before them was someone who never became overburdened and tired of the Father's will. The spiritual DNA in Jesus was coded with finishing. He wanted the disciples to know that the DNA the Holy Spirit would impart in them would do the same.

Failure was not an option. Speaking from the standpoint of genetics, Jesus was the master molecule. He was the template to measure every obedient servant. He wanted to establish a finisher's mentality in His disciples before starting their ministries.

Jesus had brought those men through a rigorous course of change. They had relinquished their wills and accepted His. There are two Greek words in the New Testament for God's will—*boulema* and *thelema*. *Boulema*[17] is the immutable, irrevocable will of God. It is accomplished whether or not we cooperate. God exercised boulema when He came in Jesus Christ to reconcile humanity. *Thelema*[18] is the desire of God, and it requires the cooperation of humans. Both words are translated into the English language as *will*. They distinguish for us the timeless application versus the operation in time. One is a settled matter before it comes to earth, and the other is the matter getting or being settled on the earth.

When we accept a learning yoke, it is for discovery. It is about discovering what has forever been settled in the heavens. It's the opportunity to venture into the eternal counsel of the

Godhead. Let me sum it up this way. Jesus had lived His life on earth yoked to the Father. It was no time to change things. Jesus' relinquishing His will in the Garden of Gethsemane was *thelema* aligning with *boulema*. **Grace, for completing his assignment, depended on this alignment**.

What does he ask the Father in His prayer? Come on, review the story in Matthew 26:39 with me! Let's put it in our language. *Is there some other way God?* Have you ever asked God that? Can we do this another way? His questions came from His humanity. But when He said, "*nevertheless*," that was the grace for the assignment talking. He did not sin by asking the question. He did not miss the mark by crying out to His Father. At that moment, Jesus felt the impact of the ages upon Him. It all converges into that moment in the Garden.

Perhaps in his humanity, sinless but human nonetheless, He was thinking within Himself that I've always been compliant. Looking at John 5:19–20 and Matthew 3, among many other verses, we know he could easily have said, "I've always been in alignment with you, Father. I don't speak anything unless I've heard you say it. I don't do anything unless I've already seen you do it. I didn't use any opportunity for self-promotion. I never used meeting people's needs as a reason to get out of compliance with the Father's will. I didn't begin in public ministry before receiving affirmation and permission."

Perhaps Jesus rehearses the last three and a half years and recalls His Father's declaration, "This is my son with whom I'm well pleased" (Matthew 3:17). Yet at the end of all things considered, He still steadfastly replies, "Is there some other way that we could do this? Nevertheless, if there is no other way to do this, not my will, but thy will be done" (Matthew 26:39; paraphrased).

The crucifixion was an aspect of God's will that He kept from the men of that age. God blinded the men of that season to assist in carrying out His will. They became the executioners of our Lord Jesus Christ.

But know this about the will of God and the will of man: None of this would have happened if Jesus did not agree to the Father's will. Yes, it looks difficult, but there will be grace to help. He kept the Father's yoke on His neck and walked it all out, joined to the Father's will—because of the joy which was set before Him, which includes you and me!

We see that Paul got a sneak peek into the agreement of the council of the Godhead. This was the mystery Paul understood:

> But we speak the wisdom of God in a mystery, even the hidden wisdom, which God ordained before the world unto our glory: Which none of the princes of this world knew: for had they known it, they would not have crucified the Lord of glory. (1 Corinthians 2:7–8)

"Herein is our love made perfect, that we may have boldness in the day of judgment: **because as he is, so are we in this world**" (1 John 4:17; emphasis added). As He is, so are we in this present age. We must stay aligned with the will and purpose of God no matter what we walk through. As the battle becomes intense, the same cry must come from us: "*Nevertheless, not my will, but thy will be done!*" Our Heavenly Father provides that same grace to us through Christ; therefore, He wants the same resolve from us. And when we respond with that resolve, as we agree with God, we manifest the life of rest in *The Savior's Perfect Yoke!*

"The Grace for completing your assignment
is engaged by your willing alignment."
— Michelle Everett
Adventure Chaplain & Catalyst for Change

Appendix

Notes

1   Strong, James. The New Strong's Expanded Exhaustive Concordance of the Bible. Red letter ed. Nashville, Tenn.: Thomas Nelson, 2010. s.v. "zygos (n)."

2   HELPS™ Word-studies copyright © 1987, 2011 by Helps Ministries, Inc.; accessed February 3, 2022; https://bibleapps.com/greek/2218.htm

3   A W Tozer, The Pursuit of God, 1948.

4   Strong, New Strong's. s.v. "moed (n)."

5   Britannica, T. Editors of Encyclopaedia. "Aratus." Encyclopedia Britannica, December 16, 2016. https://www.britannica.com/biography/Aratus-Greek-poet.

6   Strong, Augustus H, "Union with Christ," accessed February 6, 2023, https://www.monergism.com/thethreshold/sdg/union_augustus.html.

7   Strong, New Strong's. s.v. "suzugos (n)."

8   Merriam-Webster.com Dictionary, s.v. "syzygy," accessed March 30, 2022, https://www.merriam-webster.com/dictionary/syzygy.

9   Strong, New Strong's. s.v. "huperates (n)."

10   Thayer and Smith. "Greek Lexicon entry for Sklerokardia". "The NAS New Testament Greek Lexicon". 1999.

11   "H3876 - lot - Strong's Hebrew Lexicon (KJV)." Blue Letter Bible. Accessed 7 Feb, 2023. https://www.blueletterbible.org/lexicon/h3876/kjv/wlc/0-1/

12   "G1484 - ethnos - Strong's Greek Lexicon (KJV)." Blue Letter Bible. Accessed 7 Feb, 2023. https://www.blueletterbible.org/lexicon/g1484/kjv/tr/0-1/

13   "G2699 - katatomē - Strong's Greek Lexicon (KJV)." Blue Letter Bible. Accessed 7 Feb, 2023. https://www.blueletterbible.org/lexicon/g2699/kjv/tr/0-1/

14   Strong, James. The New Strong's Expanded Exhaustive Concordance of the Bible. Red letter ed. Nashville, Tenn.: Thomas Nelson, 2010. s.v. "zygos (n)."

15   Wikipedia. 2023. "Oxbow." Wikimedia Foundation. Last modified January 3, 2023. https://en.wikipedia.org/wiki/Oxbow.

16   "H8085 - šāma - Strong's Hebrew Lexicon (KJV)." Blue Letter Bible. Accessed 8 Feb, 2023. https://www.blueletterbible.org/lexicon/h8085/kjv/wlc/0-1/

17   "G1013 - boulēma - Strong's Greek Lexicon (KJV)." Blue Letter Bible. Accessed 8 Feb, 2023. https://www.blueletterbible.org/lexicon/g1013/kjv/tr/0-1/

18   "G2307 - thelēma - Strong's Greek Lexicon (KJV)." Blue Letter Bible. Accessed 8 Feb, 2023. https://www.blueletterbible.org/lexicon/g2307/kjv/tr/0-1/

Meet the Author

With over fifty years in ministry, Dr. Stephen Everett is a dynamic teacher, author, and seasoned apostolic voice. He is also the host of God's Kingdom™ a weekly television program airing earth-wide in over 163 countries.

Apostle Steve is known for imparting deep nuggets of revelation through inspiring messages that are rich and full of life. His apostolic teaching and dynamic prophetic preaching both reveal his deep passion for the maturing of The Body of Christ worldwide. He has had the honor of ministering across the USA and in fifteen other countries thus far.

This newest release in the God's Kingdom Leadership Series invites the reader to embark on a journey of discovery and dominion in the Kingdom of God. This series of books was birthed from teaching sessions during the God's Kingdom Leaders' Summits which he and his wife Michelle Everett host several times each year in various locations.

Additional works by Dr. Stephen Everett include his relevant and thought-provoking books: *God's Kingdom, The New Testament Principle of Kingdom Stewardship, The Sound that Changed Everything,* and *The Dynamic Covenant Series.*

Dr. and Mrs. Everett are the pastors of Kingdom Power & Wisdom Center and owners of Power House Studios, a Christian television studio and publishing house. They make their home in Cape Coral, Florida; together, they have nine children and five grandchildren (thus far).

To invite Dr. Stephen Everett to speak
or to purchase additional copies,
please visit :

https://drstepheneverett.org

Archived programs from his weekly
international television broadcasts are
available on demand, free of charge, at:

https://GodsKingdom.TV

Dr. Stephen Everett
Kingdom Power & Wisdom Center, Inc.
PO BOX 101678
Cape Coral FL 33910